VOICES OF DISSENT

SEAGULL
BOOKS
•
CELEBRATING
40 YEARS

THE INDIA LIST

Chittaprosad
Untitled, Scraperboard (22.9 x 25.4 cm)
Kiran Nadar Museum of Art, New Delhi; image courtesy DAG

ROMILA THAPAR

VOICES OF DISSENT
AN ESSAY

LONDON NEW YORK CALCUTTA

Seagull Books, 2023

First published by Seagull Books, 2020

This edition, 2023

© Romila Thapar, 2023

The interviews included in this edition have been reproduced with kind permission of the periodicals, newspapers and websites in which they were originally published.

ISBN   978 1 80309 270 6

British Library Cataloguing-in-Publication Data
A catalogue record for this book is available from the British Library

Typeset by Seagull Books, Calcutta, India
Printed and bound by WordsWorth India, New Delhi, India

Contents

Preface

The genesis of this essay lies in two memorial lectures that I gave in 2019 in Delhi. The first was the Nemi Chandra Jain Memorial Lecture on 'The Presence of the Other: Religion and Society in Early India', given on 16 August 2019. The second was the V. M. Tarkunde Memorial Lecture on 'Renunciation, Dissent and *Satyagraha*', given on 6 December 2019.

A friend suggested that I should combine the two as the subjects were similar. On rereading them, I thought that I could weave them together into a somewhat broader historical context. In a sense, the first provided a historical perspective on the second. So I brought them together and placed them in context. The first lecture forms the earlier part of the essay, and the second is included in the later part. In the process of doing this, I have tried to reach out to the larger historical context of the manifestations of dissent in various forms at distinctive times in the Indian past. But these are only a few examples.

Devaki Jain and Deepak Nayyar each read one of the two lectures and made helpful comments. I inflicted the larger essay on some other friends—Shirish Patel, Kunal Chakrabarti and Naveen Kishore—and again benefitted from their comments.

I am delighted that the frontispiece is a scraperboard image by Chittaprosad. For me his art had a remarkable quality. I saw many of them in the 1940s when they provided the covers for *CrossRoads*, a publication brought out by my brother Romesh Thapar.

I have in the past written on aspects of dissent in early India, but the circumstances of present times made me feel that the subject requires a more systematic perspective. The latter part of the essay is an attempt not only to relate the past to the present but also to suggest that some forms of dissent are continuities from the past. I have tried to place the subject in a bird's eye view of a historical perspective. In doing this I am trying to argue that locating dissent is not sufficient as the historian has also to indicate why such dissent had acceptability and by whom. This implies looking at forms of dissent that had public response. My focus is therefore on the question of whether this response has been fairly consistent in certain expressions of dissent.

The study of dissent is essential to understanding how civilizations evolved for there cannot be any advance in knowledge without a questioning of the world we live in.

I should add that this essay was written in the last six months—a time of extreme uncertainties—but I have tried not to let the uncertainties overwhelm me.

Romila Thapar
Delhi, September 2020

VOICES OF DISSENT

AN ESSAY

Dissent is, in essence, the disagreement that a person or persons may have with others, or, more publicly, with some of the institutions that govern their patterns of life. People have disagreed since time immemorial; they have argued, or agreed to disagree, or eventually arrived at an agreement. That is all part of life, of living. Most institutions that have an influence on our daily lives tend to have long histories; many have evolved in variant ways, and we are only now beginning to recognize that the questioning of how they function is not as recent an activity as we were imagining it to be—in fact, it has been practised for centuries.

Dissent is part of a larger body of varieties of differences that arise out of questioning and critical enquiry or just by giving vent to another experience. In writing about it, I am not downgrading other forms but trying to look more closely at those that we have neglected in our construction of the past and its culture, that which we claim to have inherited and which we acclaim in present times. Given that we continue to construct the past, the concepts we use to do so are also undergoing a similar construction. In order to explore these, it is necessary to take up leads old and new. A fuller investigation of dissent would have to examine situations where the dissent leads to protests, violent and nonviolent. My intention, however, is to make audible—symbolically—the voices of nonviolent dissent.

Dissent is not a modern concept, but recognizing it in its various forms is new, as is the fact that, in a truly liberal, democratic society, such questioning is not frowned upon but, rather, encouraged and explored through discussion. The right to question is now public, open and can be exercised by any citizen. Earlier, only the powerful had this right, but today it extends—in theory at least—to all citizens. In earlier times the right was often argued over but did not always become a public issue as it can in our times. This in part places a responsibility on us to recognize and understand the centrality of dissent. Implicit in having these rights is the exercising of dissent where we think it appropriate. This has a historical continuity even if the forms have altered. I would like to explore the continuity through a few examples.

There should always be, invariably, in every modern society, the right of the citizen to dissent as part of the right to free speech. This right has been contentious yet crucial to the continuity of societies. However much we may wish otherwise, Indian society—as indeed every other society—has not been a seamless harmonious entity, with little or no contradictions. We too have had our share of intolerance and violence and the clash of ideas. Dissenting voices have been many, and have had a much wider articulation in the past than we are willing to concede.

In historical terms, social relationships were encapsulated, as they often still are, in the binaries of those who had power and ownership—be it of land, property, rituals or whatever gives power—and those who did not. We know this relationship through conjugations such as *raja* and *praja*, the feudal lord and serf, the factory owner and employee, the colonizer and colonial subject. A couple of centuries ago, this gave way, through an overwhelming historical change, to a society that speaks of industrialization, capitalism, the middle-class control of new technology, the workers who provide the labour, the peasants on whom agricultural production depends, and such like. One of the factors that was intended to bind this new society together was nationalism, or the sense of people belonging to one nation, therefore nationhood. The massive change implicit in this, it is assumed, would be the evolving of a different relationship that determines the functioning of society. In the functioning of a nation, what matters is the relationship between the people as citizens and what they have created jointly—the state. The rights of the citizens vis-à-vis the state have therefore moved centre stage.

This historical phase also marks an alteration in the forms of governance—the earlier kingship is replaced by the emergence of democracies. Democracies can only be secular since every citizen has equal status. Their institutions have representatives from all sections of society, each having rights of equal status. This helps to integrate the secular, the democratic and the national.

In a true democracy, the right to dissent and the need to meet the demand for social justice are core concepts. Since it includes all citizens and they are legally of equal status, a democracy cannot be other than secular.

These broad historical changes have been taken as among the markers of modern times. I would like to begin, however, by discerning more general features of dissent, in terms of how dissent is recognized. Those dissenting do not always proclaim themselves as dissenters; sometimes, they may not even be fully aware of the degree to which they are dissenting. One of the more obvious ways of recognizing dissent is to mark the presence of 'the Other' in society. This facilitates recognition and juxtaposes it to dissent.

But before I write about this, I would like to clarify why I disagree with what is now often said by those who are in fact opposed to democracy but won't admit to it openly—it is said that dissent itself was imported into Indian society from the West. This is an argument made by those who visualize the Indian past as free of blemishes and therefore not requiring dissenting opinions. Such notions arise from wishful thinking. They were and are also exaggerated by descriptions of what have been called civilizations and 'high cultures', as magnificent achievements, free of fault and entirely acceptable to all those who contributed to their creation.

Civilization is said to be a moment of rare sophistication when a society virtually surpasses itself in the acme of its achievement, having followed particular paths for some centuries, guided by nascent forms. The dominant culture epitomizing civilization was thought to be superior to preceding ones. The claim maintained that there has been a prevailing acceptance of this culture by all, in a period of harmony and little contestation, both in the realm of ideas and in social activities. The characteristics of a particular civilization focused on the territory in which it was rooted, in the single dominant language in which the best of its literature and thought was written, in the single religion that gave it an identity, and in the laws that gave a structure to its functioning. This was the happy picture that the nineteenth and early twentieth century painted of world civilizations.

There were some who hinted at this being not quite accurate. While conceding the existence of ideal civilizations, they wrote of challenge and response as the pattern that created and upheld civilizations. Others wrote of the rise and decline of civilizations in inevitable historical cycles. This was not the same as dissent and disagreement but carried a hint of it. A few others suggested that when a culture achieved what could be regarded as its high point of cultural articulation there then arose alternate views about its founding features. Alternate views can take the form of indirectly supplementing what exists, or can question it. The latter can be disagreement with or dissent from the existing conventions. In whatever way one may define a culture, recognizing that there is the presence of dissent within it as the view of 'the Other' is crucial to an insightful understanding of the original.

Historians spoke of the fact that despite its having been colonized by the British and reduced to the status of a colony in modern times, India in the past had hosted a civilization with all the required characteristics. The most preferred period for this was that of the Guptas and immediately after. Indian civilization was described as a unique society of peace-loving, nonviolent people, tolerant of all and devoted to the highest ideals. There was little mention of dissenting voices. Yet, judging by the many occasions when there have been appeals for nonviolence and tolerance in the Indian past, we should recognize that Indian society also had its measure of violence and intolerance as has been the case elsewhere too. This of course is an image of the past common to many nationalists everywhere in the world of their respective homelands; or of a special quality that a particular community quotes as defining its culture—such as the concept of Negritude that gave direction to earlier African nationalisms.

What is of interest is that the knowledge on the basis of which civilization comes into being is knowledge that is frequently contested. What is conventional and conservative gets questioned, and there emerges a discourse of divergent views. This becomes clear even from a juxtaposition of different schools of thought as they existed in the 'golden ages' with the various achievements of the civilization of that period. This can also be described as a period of Classicism. But Classicism is not an innovation; rather, it is the culmination of a process that often begins in a previous age but its after-effects surface in a later—the period described as Classical. It is not altogether absent in other times and in other contexts; it simply happens to come together or is brought together more prominently in a particular age. One could well ask whether it is characteristic of such an age that there is a dialogue between those dissenting and those in authority. This is precisely what is required to advance knowledge and provide a foundation for what may still be called a civilization.

I would therefore like to look at the articulation of dissent, so essential to all societies, and consider it at various times and in varying contexts as part of the Indian historical experience. How does the Other mark its presence in Indian society in relation to 'established' society or 'the Self', to borrow a thought from Edward Said? We also need to ask about the perspective of the Other when viewing the world. I would like to regard it as a set of intertwined themes: one, the recognition of what we have begun to call the Other; and two, the interface of this Other with established society and religion, which latter is the Self. This, because it assumes the dominant position in the society that it claims it is defining. The interface naturally covers an unending range of activities but I shall take up only a few examples, focusing on inter-relations between religion and society, and the diverse relationships between the Self and the Other.

What I refer to as the Other needs explaining. Put simply: it is a person or a group of people who declare themselves to be or are recognized as different because they question some of the views of the Self. The Other or Others differ from the Self. The degree of dissimilarity varies—it can be a passing recognition of difference or it can be expressed as conscious rejection.

Whatever the degree of difference, the Other has to be recognized as present in every society. This also helps to define the identity of the Self. Like the Self, the Other has multiple aspects. So, in a contradictory way, the Other can delineate what it is opposed to and why—in other words, the Self. Those whom we see as essentially different often help us to define ourselves, both individually and socially.

Identifying people as the Other can be used for various purposes: to marginalize a section of society, to ghettoize it or even to exile it. Multiple groups all over the world in our times have become refugees by being denied citizenship or by being exiled. In the past, these rights of the citizen did not exist but today they are claimed as essential to the functioning of our societies. Treating people as the Other was not entirely unknown in the past, and often resulted in historically new cultures and aspects of a civilization. Historians recognize that what we have called civilizations were essentially porous, and textured from multiple divergent strands. The strands could be local deviant cultures or evolutions within cultures; equally often, they came with immigrants, and to a lesser extent with people of the region going out to settle elsewhere, establishing a kind of outreach or, in a few instances, even a colony. Social distancing between elite and non-elite societies was maintained through different ways of demarcating the social components, but sometimes ideas swirled up or trickled down. Existing cultures underwent change or new ones evolved. Thus, the identities of the Self and the Other could change. But the dual presence is, tacitly or otherwise, recognized in every society.

Who then determines what comprises Otherness? Those in authority generally see themselves as the established Self, and they are the ones who set up the dichotomous identity of the Self vis-à-vis the Other. Generally, it is the one who questions the Self that is described as the Other. This binary determines Otherness, helps crystallize status and power, and distances those without either. It is resorted to in most societies. But these are not permanent labels, and the relationship between the Self and the Other can change over time and move from being distanced to being proximate or the other way round. The recognition of the Other was worked into theories of social functioning over the last two centuries. Its understanding changed with colonial interpretations of Indian civilization, and is again changing now from the perspective of postcolonial times. The historical context, then, cannot be ignored in observing the relationship between the two.

People from different geographies and cultures are not the only ones thought of as the Other. More often, and to a startling degree, the Other emerges from within the same society. Since societies are stratified, socially and culturally, there is divergence—divergence caused by environment and location, economy and technology, systems of kinship and inheritance, concepts of belief and worship, and, in some cases, physical differences. These constituents of what we call culture are also defined as the pattern of living.

Because of these differences, the existence of the Other was and is inevitable. What is historically valuable is to observe how these differences shaped both the Self as well as the Other. The relationship was not inherently hostile; in practice it sometimes could be, or it need not be mutually acceptable. Where there is competition, however, the stronger tends to treat the weaker, differentiated one as the Other.

The Other was accorded a presence centuries ago in early societies, particularly wherever knowledge was being explored. At times, it lay in the presence of the shaman, the enigmatic person who was both a member of the society and an outsider. His claim was his knowledge of an inexplicable, unknown 'reality'. This was conceded by some but doubted by others.

But there were other subtle yet more comprehensible ways by which the presence of the Other was conceded. One was through argument, something that delights us all. A procedure seemingly familiar to every philosophical tradition, it hints at something akin to the dialectical method. The view of the opponent is presented; it is then countered by the view of the proponent.

This contradiction may or may not give rise to a solution. This procedure is familiar to us in Indian philosophical argument as *purvapaksha, pratipaksha* and *siddhanta*. In other schools of thought, such as the Jaina, each is segmented into finer and finer diversities, all revolving round the views of the Self and the Other.

This frame of argument has more subtle uses as well. Projecting the opposing view can also be a means of indicating what a counter-argument involves and the possibility of it being presented—it need not always be an argument that needs to be set aside. If examples of *purvapaksha* could be collected, we might have a better idea of dissenting views. Knowledge, however, cannot remain unchanging and fixed, since fresh evidence and methods of enquiry inevitably lead to its mutation. Therefore, constant questioning was and is a necessity. Given the impressive advances in knowledge—both in what might be called proto-science and in philosophy— there has been much strong and purposeful questioning in the past.

Buddhist texts mention *vivada* or contestation, which can come about through a weakness of personality— through selfishness, anger, envy, worldliness and bad intentions. But a more perceptive passage speaks of it as arising from a lack of comprehending the *dhamma* and *vinaya*—the teachings of the Buddha. At a simple level, this can mean not following the rules; at a much deeper level, it can mean questioning or contesting them. An absence of contestation would be unlikely in the context of philosophy, which assumes the questioning of the world in which we live.

In another part of the ancient world, the Socratic method suggests similar procedures. Knowledge consists of opinion and argument, and being alerted to alternatives. This leads to investigating contradictions and using reason to arrive at the truth. The method suggested by the medieval philosopher Aquinas hints at this. The original question has to be submitted to arguments both supportive and contradictory so that the question can be reconsidered fully before a reply. In modern times, philosophers changed the order somewhat and spoke of a thesis, followed by an anti-thesis, culminating possibly in a synthesis. This has become familiar to us as the dialectical method.

The presence of the Other whether as person or in the form of contradictory thought is normal to the living and thinking of any society. The Other can be accommodated through argument and discussion, and, if no resolution is forthcoming, then there can at least be an agreement to coexist. These days we are impatient with the Other and permit violent confrontation. Our impatience looms over us in many ways, often in the interface between religious and social identities. Currently, in India, it is clearly seen and heard not only in social and religious matters but in politics as well.

I should also like to briefly clarify how some of us as historians analyse the interface between society and religion. It is important to think about this, since the form of our societies and the pattern of our religions the world over were and are never accidental. They are conscious choices and therefore subject to analyses, and we must understand why we made or make these choices.

Religion is expressed at two levels—informal and formal. Informal religion has at its core the choice of the individual as to whom to worship and why and what belief to follow. It is a relatively free and personal choice. I say 'relatively' and not 'absolutely', because most of the time the decision is made for us through the link between religious and social identity. The caste and sect of the family one is born into frequently determine one's religious identity, or at least the initial one.

Religious thoughts get formalized when a belief and practice gathers followers who identify with it; it then becomes a sect. That's when the social complications begin. Founders of the sect have to impose codes of belief and social practices in order to define the sect's identity, as for example, with reference to the *dharma-shastras* and the *shari'a*. Is it the intention of the sect to conform to or to challenge such codes? The successful religion establishes institutions in society that give it authority and increase its supporters. The more obvious institutions train priests and monks, determine what goes into the canon, administer regular places of worship, organize donations, search for a guaranteed patronage, maintain formal rituals and texts, and encourage a crystallization of orthodoxy. This latter becomes the foundation of the religion and the institutions it creates, and is acknowledged by society.

Religion then comes to be seen less as drawing on individual experience and more as the articulation of a social experience or even a community. Individual belief gives way to social conformity, and the latter calls for an almost unquestioning support. At this point, there can be some differences between individual aspirations and social requirements. And this same moment may be appropriate for expressing dissent by those that do not agree with change. This is an ongoing process in the life of every formal religion and even of the larger religious sects.

Religions go through many phases with some mutation and some reformulation. Those that wish to may see it as the unfolding of a largely smooth history with the occasional glitch. In effect, what alters is determined by the historical context that registers changes from the subtle to the obvious. The original teaching, motivated by explaining human existence, can evolve through reacting to dissent or through osmosis from the proximity of other religions.

Religions founded in the name of a historically attested person have a historical trajectory beginning with the teachings of the founder and continues through various phases but with a determining teleology that may shift only slightly. Religions of another kind that are largely a coming together of various beliefs and forms of worship have moments when there is a search for a trajectory. Such searches often result in the emergence of a number of sects with somewhat varying trajectories. If there is enough social and political backing for a sect, it may claim to represent the collective. But this is of course dependent on the historical context of its emergence.

New religions may begin informally and, with increasing support, they may take on formal aspects and establish institutions to propagate their ideas and to mark their presence both in society and on the landscape. That is when we begin to notice the buildings that accompany the institutionalization of religion—*viharas, chaityas, stupas,* temples, *ashramas, mathas,* mosques, *madrassas, khanqahs,* churches, convents, *gurdwaras* and such like. Institutions change the relationship between a religion and the society in which it exists, and weaken the flexibility of the prior informal religion. The institutions are crucial to assessing the strength of the impact of a religion on society.

The form of the religion can also change when it has to play a new role in society. When this happens, it is a sign that the function of that religion is not limited to personal belief and worship. It is now in the public domain as a powerful agency involved in social and political policies. At this point the interconnection between religion and society registers immense complexity.

When codes of belief and social practice are established, and orthodoxies come into existence, this is when dissent becomes a possibility, and sometimes even a necessity in the opinion of some. Every formal religion and mature society faces dissenters. Dissent then, in an inverted way, furthers orthodoxy if the latter tries to curb dissent. The Other differs from the orthodoxy. It has its own formal belief and organization evolving from this difference. Orthodoxy then has a choice: the supporters of dissenting ideas can be excluded and opposed as the enemy within society, or their dissent can be diluted by treating them as yet another sect among many, or else dissent can lose its identity by being gradually assimilated. Until colonial times, religion as practised in India had a greater propensity for this Otherness. The forms it took were more as sects that spoke to large numbers of people rather than the limited social elite. The interface of society and religion therefore became central.

In situations of historical change, these relations could also undergo change, and in some exceptional cases, even be reversed. We should also keep in mind that cultures—by which I mean patterns of living—are never homogenous, unalloyed or static. There is no pristine, pure culture that continues as such throughout history. Every culture mutates either through its own evolving impetus or through the entry of new elements. This is part of the reason why the relationships between orthodoxy and heterodoxy can also vary and are susceptible to historical change. A religion has multiple roots and multiple branchings-off, and this ensures its immortality.

Historical change can alter these relationships. The history of a religion or a society is never static. In India, religions as practised by people at large tended not to be monolithic or uniform across the subcontinent except at some elite levels. In pre-colonial times, religious identities were expressed more frequently through sects, either based on a large caste or one cutting across castes. These spoke to specific social categories and generally to a wider audience than just the elite. It is crucial therefore to know which section of society a sect is addressing.

All this is by way of a general introduction. Let me turn now to my examples. But before I do so, let me explain why my examples come from forms of dissent that pertain to religions. The public forum for discussion in pre-modern times in India was often discussions on various aspects of prevalent religions. This cannot be attributed to a pre-eminence of religious thought in all things but, rather, to religion being the broader idiom through which much else was discussed, such as the attribution of social status, the legitimizing of political authority and the control over economic assets. In earlier times, some religions did connect beliefs and actions appropriate to the functioning of society, such as the linking of caste to religious ritual. In pre-modern societies, the assertion of power, as indeed also the questioning of power, is often articulated through religious ideas. At many levels these are the agencies of power.

Some have argued that there were no dissenting groups in the history of Hinduism, because it was a tolerant religion and accepted all points of view. The fact that there were dissenting points of view suggests the opposite and there is of course evidence of religious confrontations. I have argued that religious loyalties in India generally draw much more on the innumerable religious sects, some of which have very tenuous links to the more established religions. The immediate identity was more often that of the sect. Tolerance is better measured by observing the ongoing relationships between sects. There is evidence of both casual and sometimes more severe dissent in all religions.

Where religion is closely tied to social status and social identity as through its links with caste differences— and these were prevalent in all the main Indian religions with marginal differences—the fundamental relationship between those with caste status / *varna* and those without it / *avarna* raises other questions. Is a religion using double standards if in its teaching it maintains that every human being is equal yet in its practice makes distinctions? Correlating the religious ideal with the functioning of social reality can be problematic. This is so in most religions, and in some the ethical question is posed but remains unanswered.

My focus is not in tracing the ideas that went into the construction of dissent. These have been studied in the philosophical perspectives of various religions of the subcontinent. My attempt is to try and understand why a certain kind of Other received such a ready and substantial response from the public, both in the past and in modern times. The reason for this response is worthy of further thought. The dissenting message of these kinds of Others was recognized and frequently supported. This may tell us more about the role of dissent in Indian cultures, a role that we tend to dismiss or to underplay.

I would like initially to take up three differing examples from our pre-modern history, and comment on how the Other was perceived in each and on how dissent was expressed and recorded. I shall restrict myself to northern India with which history I am more familiar, and shall take my examples from three different millennia. My choice has been with reference to religion in a broad sense because religion when used as ideology motivates supporters to also follow a social pattern. The interface between religion and society illumines both. I shall then discuss a modern form that drew from the context of the previous ones. These will also suggest the perceptions that we, as the obsessive present, have of the past, and observe the interface that once existed.

*

1. *The* Dasyah-putrah Brahmana, *or the* Dasi-putra Brahmana, *the* Brahmana *Who Is the Son of a* Dasi

My first example of the Other goes back to the second millennium BC to Vedic times. This is an example of the Other being from a different culture. From the language sources that we have of these times, the dominant religion was based on the *Vedas* as practised and taught by *brahmanas* and thought to be unique to them. However, mention is made of the presence of Others as well, a presence that is conceded by us casually, since the stronger articulation is that of the one dominant culture. The popular view today, insisting that there was only one dominant culture, faintly acknowledges the presence of other cultures. The story from the side of the Other remains largely uninvestigated or seldom told. This may be because it complicates an otherwise straightforward narrative.

The *Rigveda* refers frequently to distinct peoples, and one recurrent classification is the dual division into the *arya varna* and the *dasa* and *dasyu*. The *arya*, from which Max Müller and others gave currency to the word 'Aryan', were those that were respected as persons of status who spoke correct Sanskrit and practised the Vedic religion. Language was the key to identity and this incorporated status.

For many centuries, the word *arya* remained the qualifier of a superior social category. However, the identification of Aryan became axiomatic in the nineteenth century when race became a primary factor in the colonial understanding of the people it had colonized. The idea of an Aryan race goes back a couple of centuries from the present and arose from equating the cultural idiom of language—the Aryan speech—with the altogether different factor of biological birth: an erroneous equation. As we are all well aware, the notion of race determining a culture anywhere in the world was discarded well over half a century ago. It is incorrect to speak of an Aryan race and yet the phrase keeps coming up in popular parlance.

We know about the culture of the *arya* from detailed descriptions in the Vedic corpus. But who then was the *dasa*? Evidently the Other of the *arya*, since the term is often used in that sense. Not unexpectedly, the first distinction is that of language. Those that cannot speak the Vedic language correctly or not at all are dismissed as *mridhra-vac*, of hostile or incorrect speech, and later the term *mleccha* is used for those who speak incorrectly amid other failings. Much fun is made of those who invariably replace the *r* sound by the *l* sound. These *mleccha* would have been inhabitants of the Ganges plain because this sound replacement continues in this region for many centuries. It is present, for instance, in a few versions of some inscriptions of the Mauryan king Ashoka from this region dating to the third century BC, where *raja magadhe* is written as *laja magadhe*. If everyone had been an Aryan speaker in origin, then such mistakes would have been less likely.

Language is an immediate identity. Being alien is encapsulated in the term *amanusha*. What were the other unambiguous differences? They practised a different religion, therefore were called *adeva*, without gods, and did not perform the required *yajnas* / ritual sacrifices, not even the important *soma* rituals. The *soma* ritual was a characteristic of those *aryas* whose language was Old Iranian and Old Indo-Aryan, suggesting closeness in language, ritual and culture. But worse, not only were the *dasas* phallic worshippers but earned further disapproval for this since the *aryas* did not worship icons. The rituals of the *aryas* generally precluded the worship of icons. The *dasas* had access to magic as also did the *yatudhana* and the *rakshasa*, so they are disliked with an element of fear, but there is a hint of envy too, associated as they seem to have been with some inexplicable power. The *dasas* were described sometimes as unfriendly, greedy and socially rather unacceptable.

However, the relationship was complicated. Some *dasas* were wealthy, especially in herds of cattle, and therefore were subjected to cattle raids. Hustling cattle was a regular activity. The *dasas* lived in settlements with stockades, the *purs*. These we are told were attacked by the *aryas* with the help of the gods Indra and Agni. The *dasas* were divided into clans / *vish*, each headed by a chief. An occasional chief may have been a patron of the Vedic ritual sacrifices. Fees, after all, especially from wealthy patrons are always welcome. Where the *dasas* are described as enemies, their numbers are given in exaggeratedly large figures. This is not unexpected since accounts of hostilities in ancient sources tend to exaggerate the enemy numbers.

So who were these *dasas* who figure so prominently as the Other? Their identification remains problematic. Archaeology provides evidence of a number of sites of diverse cultures but their identities as communities remain unclear, barring the sites that carry traces of post-Harappan culture. The peninsula has a distinctly different culture in the Megalithic sites scattered across it.

What the Vedic corpus seems to suggest is that this intriguing relationship between the *arya* and the *dasa* had its own history. It began with the *dasas* who, being seemingly indigenous, were initially treated by the incoming *aryas* as having an alien culture. But gradually, social divisions within the *dasa* society, as indicated in the texts, made for varied relationships with the *aryas*. Not all *dasas* were wealthy. Those that were may have been inducted into *arya* society, whereas the impoverished ones remained in servile occupations.

As usual, the women were the more impoverished ones. *Dasi* women are treated as chattel by wealthy *aryas* and gifted to others by *arya* chiefs. They are occasionally listed together with horses and cattle as part of the wealth that was gifted, presumably from the loot acquired after a cattle raid. In the *arya* community the *dasi* remains a commodity. *Dasis* work in *arya* households. This would also be true of the many *dasas* reduced to servitude and distanced socially. It is sometimes said of agro-pastoral communities that when they raid the wealth of sedentary communities, they capture the women and bring them home. They can then either be wives or work in the household as servants and slaves. Women of the *dasa* community working in the household would have been referred to as *dasis*.

But curiously, some of the sons of these *dasis* are given high status and are referred to literally as *dasyah-putrah brahmana,* or *dasi-putra brahmanas,* that is, *brahmanas* who are the sons of *dasis*. What are we told about this particular category of *brahmanas*? Some of the highly respected ones are mentioned by name with stories woven round them. The *rishi* Dirghatamas is consistently known by his metronymic, Mamateya, hinting at a different kinship system from the usual *arya* patriarchy. He was clearly special because he is said to have anointed the great raja, Bharata. He married a *dasi,* Ushija. The revered *rishi* Kakshivant, whose hymns are included in the *Rigveda*, also had a mother of the same name and chose to take his mother's name and is called Aushija. A slightly later text, the *Brihad-devata*, refers to him as the son of Dirghatamas and his *dasi* wife Ushija. This would have made him a *brahmana* who was the son of a *dasi*. Was a *dasi* mother just a matter of low status, or a mark of being from a different culture?

The equally renowned sage Kavasha Ailusha was also the son of a *dasi*. It is said of him in the *Aitareya Brahmana* that he was driven away from a *soma* sacrifice by the regular *brahmanas* because of his birth. As he wandered away, he recited some verses and the river Saraswati began to follow him. Seeing this, the regular *brahmanas* immediately recognized that he was special to the gods, so they welcomed him back, gave him *brahmana* status, and more, they declared him to be the best among *brahmanas*. What was his special power that despite his mother being a *dasi* he was honoured by the *brahmanas*?

The *Chandogya Upanishad* carries the story often quoted of Satyakama Jabala who came to the *rishi* Gautama requesting that he be accepted as a student to study the *Vedas*. The *rishi* asked him if he was a *brahmana*. He replied that his mother had told him that she worked as a *dasi* in a household and she could not recall who his father may have been. The *rishi* replied that who but a *brahmana* would have told the truth as Satyakama had done, and he was accepted as a student. Here the *varna* identity gave way to an ethical qualification.

Despite having *dasi* mothers, these particular *rishis* perfected their knowledge of the language of the *aryas* and moved easily among them. Born to mothers of the lowest status, they were recruited into the highest caste and were not described as *mridhra-vac* or *mleccha*; but nor were they given any lineage connections that would have allowed them to claim a high status. Is there a hint here of a subtle and new socio-religious interface of a more complex kind that needs further investigation and that may reflect on the early forms of society and status?

The *dasa* culture is the culture of the Other. Keeping this in mind, a careful reading of the *Rigveda* brings up evidence of the presence of the *dasa* as being more than just marginal, even if the hymns are primarily concerned with the rituals and beliefs of the *arya*. The term itself, the *brahmana* who is the son of a *dasi*, suggests a special category of *brahmanas* who, even if recruited from a substratum culture, are prized for some magical or powerful ritual knowledge that they appear to have had. Can we infer from this that the *brahmana* caste did incorporate individuals or groups of various origins, wherever it thought appropriate—a process that is not altogether unfamiliar from later times? Do we then have to search the Vedic corpus for aspects that may have derived from *dasa* culture? This would require comparative studies of these other contemporary cultures in greater depth than has been done so far.

One sees in these references the gradual merging of some aspects of various groups, modifying their identities. If a *dasa* learnt the language of the *arya* would this mean that he had been 'Aryanized'? On demonstrating his superior power, the *dasa*'s superiority was acknowledged and the *arya*, it would seem, sought to appropriate it. Did some of the *dasa* culture rub off even marginally onto the *arya*? Or was there a more nuanced mutation in both? We also need to remember that if this was so, then this activity would most likely have been limited to the higher castes. The majority, consisting of the lower castes and those outside caste, were subsequently, according to orthodox opinion, not even allowed to hear the recitation of the *Vedas*. They would have had other deities to worship and in ways different from the rituals of the *yajnas*.

These sons of *dasis* are not described as *nastika* / non-believers, since there seems to be some eagerness to acquire their knowledge. However, the *astika* : *nastika* differentiation of believer : non-believer, is made with reference to a range of teachings and of philosophical ideas of another kind. In this connection it would be worth trying to ascertain the point at which heterodoxy confronts the thinking of those regarded as the orthodox. The question has been asked as to whether the *nastika* and the heterodox can be equated. A distinction can be made in that the non-believer is so labelled with reference to the issue of belief in deity and its consequences, whereas heterodoxy is the wider rejection of the fundamentals of an orthodoxy. Presumably, the recognition that some did not agree and were non-believers would indicate this point of difference. Literally, *nastika* is more than just atheism in its reference to the absence of deity, as it refers to the rejection of the belief of those propagating a belief in deity. The contempt for the non-believer comes only from the believer, and specific believers at that, and cannot be taken as a general view.

Did this duality and the occasions when it may have been omitted create a new culture that drew from both sources? There are references to categories of the Others, as, for instance, those that observe different customs.

The Asuras, for example, do not cremate their dead but bury them. The Vratyas, culturally distinct from the *aryas* but speaking the language, are finally admitted to the *arya* fold by performing a special ritual. Were they the fallen ones because they had moved away from Vedic rituals? Were such rituals necessary for other non-*aryas* as well for them to be admitted to the *arya* fold? Or was there a distinction between those that had the potential to be admitted and those that lacked it?

Unfortunately, we have no sources to tell us how the *dasa* community viewed the *aryas,* and more especially the *brahmanas.* Some strands of Upanishadic thought, much later than the *Rigveda,* have been attributed to possible non-Vedic authors by modern commentators. Was this why its ideas were initially held as a secret doctrine? The *kshatriya* chiefs of some of the clans, distinct from the *brahmana* teachers, are suggested as authors of some of these doctrines. The schools of thought and practice had now grown larger in number. The antecedents of these sects and the cultures they represent remain intriguing questions.

Other texts also mention the sons of *dasis* in *arya* households, but they are not given the status of *brahmanas* even when born of *brahmana* fathers. In the *Mahabharata,* for instance, Vidura, the son of Vyasa and a *dasi*, plays a noticeable role. His comments on various events reflect or hint at a dissenting opinion. But he was never given high status. The presence specifically of *brahmanas* as the sons of *dasis* suggests the interface of cultures and a dialogue between the Self and the Other and the possible accommodation of some dissenting views. These specific *brahmanas* were not those who dissented and went their own way; on the contrary, they came from a culture that was regarded as the Other but were nevertheless incorporated into *brahmana* status. It was a form of inducting those that came from the culture of the Other.

*

2. The Presence of the Shramanas

Let me now turn to my second and rather different example: an existing culture gives rise to an alternative Other from within itself. The Other here was not regarded as being of an alien culture but, evolving out of a similar culture, was nevertheless dissenting from the codes of dominant groups. I am taking you now into the early ADs, to the emergence of groups that were a different Other and were jointly called the Shramanas—these were the Jainas, Buddhists and Ajivikas. Some would include the Charvakas / Lokayatas as well, although their thinking was very different.

The teachings of the Shramanas revolved round each of their historical founders. The Buddhists, for example, accepted the Buddha, the *dhamma* / *dharma* and the Sangha as the pillars of their teaching. They had fewer elaborate public rituals and used discussion or texts when stating their principles. They had a few demarcated places of worship, the *chaityas* and *stupas*. The latter held the relics of the venerated dead, contrary to Vedic practice.

The question of *ahimsa* / nonviolence was central to the teaching of the Buddhists and Jainas. This was not so in the texts endorsed by Brahmanism nor in its rituals of sacrifice. It became a matter of debate, as is reflected in various texts such as the *Mahabharata* and the *Bhagavad-Gita*. Where violence is permitted if it is against evil, as in the *Gita*, the issue becomes somewhat ambivalent.

Who decides that certain actions are evil and opposed to the code of ethics—the Self or the Other? (I shall refer to this discussion again later.) The Buddha's emphasis on *karuna* / compassion reflects what was being said about this by various teachers. The emphasis on *ahimsa* is underlined more frequently in Shramanic teaching than in the other. Of the Vedic corpus, the *Upanishads* are perhaps more open to these discussions.

The Charvakas were not Shramanas and on occasion their views conflicted. They not only denied the existence of deity but extended this denial to all that cannot be verified. Atheism, rationalism and the need to question was not heresy, it was a right exercised by thinking people. The search was for explaining the real world. We are responsible for our actions and are aware of the consequences. These occur in this life as there is no rebirth. Rituals were rejected and dismissed. A number and variety of such groups debated these ideas and the liveliness sometimes led to entanglements of thought. That is why the Buddha referred to some among them as 'eel-wrigglers'.

The Shramanas were opposed in varying degrees to Vedic Brahmanism. They questioned the belief in deities, in the *Vedas* being divinely revealed, in the efficacy of the *yajna* / ritual of sacrifice, and in the existence of the individual soul or *atman*. Brahmanical literature refers to the Shramanas categorically as *nastika*, the non-believers, the *astika* being the believers. This duality of belief and non-belief remained fundamental to the

Brahmanical view of itself and of non-brahmanical religions. It should be differentiated from other dualities in Indian thought. As a term for non-brahmanical belief and practice, *nastika* continued to be used through the centuries. The concept was not limited to religious thought and it would obviously have carried a social message as well. If deity could be doubted, then so could the laws that were made in the name of the deities as well as the claim of communication between men and gods.

These opposed ideologies underwent many changes as they meandered their way through history. The persons associated with the founding of the more important Shramana religions were from the upper castes, as were many initial followers. Shramanism was open to lower castes who could become lay followers and monks. Rituals were less dramatic than the Vedic ones and were not tied to caste status. Abiding by caste norms was not a criterion of admission to their ranks and the existence of caste was not essential to their teaching. Their dissent was more in the nature of opposing beliefs rather than restructuring society, although the latter was not marginal to their thinking and some restructuring was inevitable. The continuance of caste could be problematic since social ethics was implicit to Shramanic thinking. However, even for the post-Vedic formal religions that evolved around Shaivism and Vaishnavism, the Shramanas were the *nastika* Others. That Puranic religion was facing a threat is apparent from the mention in the *Puranas* of dissenters who question the *Vedas* through false arguments and who can be recognized by their red robes, a reference to the robes worn by the Shramana monks.

Apart from their differences of belief religious sects were competitors for royal patronage in the form of donations to their institutions and later there were grants of land to maintain these institutions. Patronage kept the Shramana sects going and gave them a place in society. The competition would doubtless have added to the ideological hostility. The patrons of the Shramanas included a large segment of society such as householders owning land or *gahapatis*, and wealthy merchants or *setthis*, mercantile guilds and craftsmen and their families, apart from the gradually increasing royal patronage. Their popularity extended to wider levels of society and that would doubtless have added to their ideological differences with Brahmanism.

Various historical sources refer to two streams of what might be called religion, two *dharmas* visible on the historical scene. To list a few here : Megasthenes visited Mauryan India in the fourth century BC, coming from the neighbouring Hellenistic Seleucid kingdom in West Asia. He wrote an account of his visit, the *Indika*. In this he speaks of the seven castes of Indian society of which the highest is divided into two: the Brachmanes and the Sarmanes / the Brahmanas and the Shramanas. The Shramanas, described as philosophers, are not included among the Brahmanas but are listed as distinctive and separate. The edicts of the Mauryan emperor

Ashoka issued in the third century BC make repeated pleas for harmony between the various sects. These are often included in the compound phrase in Prakrit *bahmanam-samanam* when speaking of the sects. The Sanskrit grammarian Patanjali, writing just before the Christian era, compares the antagonism between the *brahmana* and the Shramana to that between the snake and the mongoose.

That the differentiation between the two increased over the centuries is apparent from a text that evokes the idea of a conversion to the Buddhist *dhamma*. Nagasena, a Buddhist monk claims to be recording his conversation about Buddhism with the Indo-Greek king Menander in his text *Milinda-panho / The Questions of King Menander*. The questions posed and the answers given are fascinating inasmuch as they draw variously on belief and rational argument. So far no comparable text has been found from the Brahmanical tradition. Perhaps this illustrates one of the fundamental differences between the two in their approach to religion. The *brahmana* would have regarded Menander as a *mleccha* and kept him away from participating in the rituals or would have had to bestow upper-caste status on him, whereas the Buddhist was anxious to recruit him as he was, as a Buddhist lay follower.

Clearly, there were by now many sects with dissenting views. No religion was uniformly observed, nor was it strictly monolithic in its teaching. The two significant traditions of thought are frequently referred to in the sources. This is further confirmed in the early *Puranas* where hostile remarks on the Shramanas indicate the antagonism between the two. Al-Biruni describes the Brahmana religion at length but also mentions those that are opposed to it as the Sammaniyas.

In the period between the Mauryas and the Guptas, there is a striking presence of impressive Buddhist *stupas,* and an equally striking absence of temples, a situation that was slowly reversed in the subsequent post-Gupta period. Religious buildings are among the indicators of patronage and popularity. It was a time of intense social change with clan societies giving way to caste societies and many kingdoms being established in areas where earlier there had been clan assemblies, or minimal governmental control, or even none at all. Possibly, it could be said that it was a period when the Shramanas were the more established Selves as it were, and the emerging Puranic Hinduism was a competitor— a position that was reversed in the post-Gupta period. Was the Buddhist *Dhammapada* facing the *dharma-shastras* of Brahmana authorship more centrally than before? The vision of universal concerns was being slowly recast into the restricted concerns of a caste-bound society.

It was subsequent to this that the Buddhists and Jainas, described as heretics and dissidents in the *Puranas* of the early centuries AD, began to experience persecution. It seemed to coincide with increasing royal patronage being bestowed on *brahmanas*. The hostility of Shaiva sects against the Shramanas finds mention, whether in Kashmir or in Tamil Nadu. Buddhist monks and monasteries were attacked in Gandhara as stated in the *Rajatarangini* of Kalhana, and Jaina monks met a similar fate elsewhere. Why this was so has still to be convincingly explained. Was it just a conflict over patronage between the Puranic and Shramana religions?

The Shramana religions were facing their own internal divisions. Buddhism was split into two major schools —the Mahayana / Greater Vehicle, and the Hinayana / Lesser Vehicle. The former had a marked presence in north-western India and Central Asia. Innumerable sects emerged and, based on belief and practice, were connected loosely or firmly to the school of their choice. In subsequent centuries, further schools were added, such as the Vajrayana, influenced by the Tantric religion.

Buddhism tended to be active in a few pockets and more so in eastern India, although for a shorter period. It gradually faded from being foremost among the Shramana religions having conceded ground to the idea of deity and related practices. Its decline was furthered by other socioeconomic changes. A decline in commerce doubtless affected its patronage as did the diversion of royal donations elsewhere. The argument that Islam dealt a death-blow to Buddhism in India is untenable since Buddhism had ceased to be pre-eminent even before the coming of Islam to North India. This is suggested by the assessment of the seventh-century AD Chinese Buddhist monk Xuanzang, who travelled widely in India and eventually spent a few years studying in Nalanda.

As a contrast to Buddhism's quietude in India, this was the period when it had a spectacular following in most parts of Asia. Buddhist missionary activity marked a major difference from other Indian religions that tended to be stay-at-home. Buddhist monks pioneered missions to Central Asia in the early centuries AD, travelling with the merchants active in establishing trade links along many routes that have come to be called the Silk Routes. They also travelled along the maritime trade routes through South-East Asia. Curiously, Puranic Hinduism that also did a modicum of travelling at this time, and through the same channels as Buddhism, remained a marginal religion if at all in most places. In South-East Asia it offered some competition initially but eventually gave way to Buddhism.

The Jainas survived perhaps by consolidating their patronage and rooting themselves in specific areas such as Karnataka and Western India, supported substantially by the wealthy mercantile community and occasionally by royalty. The teaching was largely split into two major schools, the Digambara and the Shvetambara, each with many sects. Their monasteries became centres of scholarship focusing on their own teaching and thus forming a kind of counterpart to the *mathas* of the *brahmanas*. Many had a proficiency in accounting and finance that linked them to the commercial activities of those times and to the lives of trading communities. Possibly some concession was made here or there in ritual and worship, as in the spectacular temples they built, that indicated their well-being. This again has to be examined.

Among the philosophical Others that we often dismiss were the materialist philosophers of the Charvaka teaching. They are neglected because of our obsession with the idea that India has only respected non-materialist philosophies in the past. Unfortunately, there is no surviving text of major significance that they authored on their philosophy, much of it being taught orally. Had there been some texts, then they would have been given greater space. There are, however, references to them and summaries of their teachings in diverse texts. Some regard the *Arthashastra* as a text that shows traces of Charvaka thinking. This may be because Kautilya underlines the importance of critical enquiry, with an emphasis on *tarka* / logic. This may suggest that dissent was latent in various schools of Indian thought and we have to be more sensitive to its presence.

In the *Mahabharata*, a *rakshasa* named Charvaka upbraids Yudhishthira on the futility of the killing that resulted from the battle at Kurukshetra. He is silenced when he is himself killed by the *brahmanas* present. Buddhist texts were also not, on the whole, friendly towards the Charvakas, even though the teaching of both was opposed to that of the *brahmanas*. Gradually, there developed a tendency for Brahmanical texts to list the non-Brahmanical schools altogether in one list and describe them all as *nastika* / non-believers.

However, it would seem that Charvaka thinking was present through the centuries to medieval times. A compendium of current fourteenth-century philosophies, the *Sarva-darshana-samgraha,* written by Madhavacharya, a philosopher of the time, has as its opening chapter a discourse on Charvaka philosophy. The author explains that although he himself did not agree with its arguments, it was nevertheless a known school of thought. This suggests that the philosophy of materialism was present both among philosophers and others. We are also told that when Emperor Akbar invited representatives of various philosophical schools, the Charvakas were one among them. We need to restore them to their rightful place in our assessment of the philosophical spectrum in Indian thought. Even if this is not stated directly, they are likely to have been in dialogue with the other streams, else they would have faded out before the fourteenth century. Of the two main streams, the dialogue of the Charvakas would more likely have been with the Shramanas.

So much by way of a very brief sketch of the background.

Dissent that uses the idiom of religion, as did many pre-modern dissenting groups, did not confine itself to writing dissenting texts. It is not enough to look only at the texts that resulted from conflicting ideas, although this is a necessary step. These provide some of the explanation that gave rise to dissent. It is equally important to study the institutions that religious groups built to support their activities and through which conformity or dissent was expressed. In some instances, these had more than a marginal role in formulating either the one or the other. I shall refer to just a few examples to illustrate the point.

The Shramanas established a new personality on the social landscape—that of the renouncer. This entity occasionally took on the characteristics of a counter-culture. It was a new kind of Other. The renouncers as monks lived separately in their own institutions—the monasteries that were sometimes identified by sect. They were dependent on society for alms, mainly food. They broke the rules of caste by being celibate, by eating cooked food given by anyone irrespective of caste, and (in theory at least) by not segregating the *savarna*, those belonging to a *varna* / caste, from the *avarna*, those without a *varna* identity. The well-established sects among these intervened in politics and social concerns although claiming to be focused on religion, a situation that continues to this day in the nexus between many religious sects and politics and in the political activities of religious organizations. Patronage is frequently the link. The renouncer opting out of society but claiming to have the welfare of society as his concern acquires a degree of moral authority within society, and this can increase in accordance with his teaching and activity. This was a feature of pre-modern times and, as we shall see, is not unknown to modern times as well.

In order to maintain the institutions of the renouncers, the granting of land and large donations towards their maintenance continued. It enabled them to become powerful social and political institutions but their role as Others gradually diminished. Donations to *brahmanas* as individuals or as groups or as institutions helped in building up a strong religious base for Brahmanism, as had earlier been so for Buddhism. The institutionalizing of a religion inevitably gives it a certain control over secular functioning. It subsumes the secular into the religious authority. The multitude of inscriptions from the late first millennium AD recording grants of land and wealth donated to *brahmanas* gave to Brahmanism a larger political and economic status than merely the role of ritual specialists conducting Vedic sacrificial and other rituals, building temples and worshipping icons placed therein. Inevitably the religion itself underwent a shift.

The success of Brahmanism in unsettling the Shramanas was in part due to *brahmanas* now receiving a large share of patronage. Royal patronage to Vedic Brahmanism continued but had also to adjust to the growing demands of the institutions of a form of Hinduism that might be better referred to as Puranic Hinduism. This was the worship of various manifestations of Vaishnavism and Shaivism to begin with and later included the Shakta-Shakti and other cults. Within these larger assemblages were included on occasion some local deities inducted into the Puranic pantheon. When this happened, the ritual specialists either became a separate caste category or were drawn into the *brahmana* caste. Evidence of this is more common after the Gupta period. In some ways it is minimally reminiscent of the *brahmana* sons of *dasis* being given *brahmana* status. Local deities could be from another tradition, but if it was expedient to induct them into Puranic Hinduism, it was done.

In fact, Puranic Hinduism, although it invokes Vedic Brahmanism, was in many respects distinct. Some of its major features suggest a reaction to the competition with Shramanism. This would be an example of dissent helping to engineer a new formulation of an existing religion. Its texts were the *Puranas*, composed in a more widely spoken Sanskrit than the now-rather-archaic Vedic Sanskrit of the *Vedas*, and in later centuries even more in local languages. The study and recitation of the *Vedas* was restricted to appropriate people, but the *Puranas* were recited and made familiar to popular audiences. Unlike the major Vedic sacrificial rituals that were not associated with the worship of idols and could be performed wherever thought suitable, and whose locations were disbanded at the conclusion of the ritual, Puranic Hinduism now began building permanent places of worship, namely, temples housing images of deities with an increasing focus on their worship, and accompanying the changes in the religion. These innovations are reflected in the late *dharma-shastras* where, for example, there is a discussion on which *brahmana* is to be given priority—the one who is a specialist in the *Vedas* or the temple priest.

Beginning as places housing icons being worshipped, temples were to gradually become immensely large and complex institutions supported by the offerings of the worshippers and the donations of land and money by wealthy patrons. All this had to be administered by a large body of priests. They also became major places of pilgrimage, and with gatherings of people from a variety of places, they doubled up as commercial centres that in turn gave them an added economic importance.

The Shramanas had their institutions that impinged on society in the form of *viharas* / monasteries, *chaityas* / halls of worship and *stupas* / relic mounds. Puranic Hinduism had its institutions that were entirely different in the form of temples and of *mathas* / centres of textual religion and learning. That religious institutions were extending their reach over the socioeconomic and political activities of the time becomes evident. This brought about a change from earlier times in the inter-relation between religion and society. It was no longer limited to religion providing a path to worship, since it now extended to religious institutions intervening in the activities of society. Patronage was absolutely crucial to the continuance of these socio-religious institutions.

There was a gradual shift in patronage, especially among royal families with greater support going to the *brahmanas* who by now were increasingly the authors and the ritual specialists of Puranic Hinduism. Two obvious factors might explain this change. The *brahmanas* could supply the upstart dynasties with lineage links to ancient *kshatriya* genealogies to legitimize their being called the new *kshatriyas* as many were; and the claim of the *brahmanas* that they could perform effective rituals to avert evil and bad luck in order to ensure the continuous and successful rule of these dynasties.

Coinciding with this, patronage from wealthy merchants and guilds to the Shramana institutions possibly declined in this period when there was a fall in trade and wealth to donate was not easily available. Monasteries and trading groups had a close connection with the former, sometimes as participants in commercial activities. Changes in the volume of trade would therefore decrease the patronage available to monasteries and thereby curtail their activities.

Nevertheless, this period saw substantial scholarship both among the Shramanas and the *brahmanas* in a remarkable articulation of philosophical ideas. Given that the premises of each were so different, there was naturally much debate that drew on both orthodoxy and dissent. Dissent was not restricted to the instituting of renunciatory orders. It also focused on the discussion of philosophical ideas. Debates were known to take place at royal courts, as, for instance, at that of Harshavardhana, the seventh-century ruler of Thanesar-Kanauj. Among the well-known philosophers of around that period were Dignaga and Dharmakirti. Subsequently, the practice is associated with Shankaracharya and others.

Even within what may broadly be called the different Shramana traditions, there evolved a large range of sects that differed among themselves and asserted a degree of autonomy. The differences focused on the interpretation of the teachings of the founders, on the rules of the monastic orders, and on the precepts required to be observed by lay followers. Such differences could be theological in origin or more often due to a changing historical context.

For instance, when the money economy gained currency in early times, an obvious question arose as to whether monks could accept donations of money, and this was one of the causes of a rift in the early Buddhist Sangha. Later when patrons and donors included more than just the lay following and registered gifts from diverse categories such as royalty and mercantile interests, the particular requirements of each of these categories had to be accommodated. Large donations of land generally from royalty led to what Max Weber described as monastic landlordism. This was counter to the rule that the monastery should not own property, and more so when the landed property was so large that it required the monks to do administrative work and supervise the labour employed to work the land. In such situations, the monastery was also a socioeconomic institution not entirely divorced from political connections. As such its nurturing of dissent might have been muted. The imprint of having to administer landed property would also have altered the patterns of living in the *mathas* and *agraharas* of the *brahmanas*, not to mention the richly endowed temples. Not all *brahmanas* could spend their time studying the texts, for some among them had to supervise the farming and its ancillary produce and some others had to keep the accounts in order. The monks of the monasteries were familiar with these procedures.

From the mid-first millennium AD, the Shramanic religions were not invariably dissenting groups in relation to the increasingly well-endowed Puranic Hinduism. By this time, they had evolved both their own orthodoxies and their own dissenting ideas and practices vis-à-vis these orthodoxies. The survival of these varied.

Virtually every religion in India consisted by now of multiple sects, each seeking its own patronage and asserting its identity. This pattern was applicable to later religions as well. Having an institution and an identity helped in locating it in the gamut of sects and this allowed it to be characterized as conforming to or dissenting from, or locating itself somewhere in-between the original teaching and its variant. The feasibility of differences and their coexistence was recognized, although some among them faced animosity and conflict. But in either case, the relationship between sects, whether friendly or hostile, was confined to small, local groups. A single, uniformly applicable, overarching religion was unfamiliar. Nor was there a single sacred overarching text even for what might be taken as a formal religion. A canon was recognized by some of the followers but no text was singled out as unquestionably the single and most sacred one over and above all others. This made the localization of religious practices and ideas far stronger than the somewhat abstract loyalty to an over-arching single text.

Later when attempts were made to write on past events linked to the religion, these tended to be potted histories or documented recalls of the sect rather than a story of the larger religion. Even where they began with the larger story, they moved into the particulars of the sect. The Shramana religions had better documentation on their pasts but this may have been because they were rooted in the thoughts of a historical founder, and they were initially dissident groups that made it a point to construct and recall the past, perhaps in part to give themselves legitimacy. One of the purposes of claiming a history is to claim legitimacy. Today, however, we require that the history not be a casual narrative, but be such that it draws on reliable evidence for supporting the claim.

Interestingly, this was also a time when the notion of heresy was spoken of more frequently in a variety of texts, such as the *Puranas*. This is significant since the *Puranas* were the texts that gave a formal structure to Puranic Hinduism. Heresy takes on a force when dissent from a canonical position becomes apparent and audible, when a lay following and competition for patronage increases, and when the institutional base of orthodoxy requires larger investments of wealth.

The success of Brahmanism in the later first millennium meant that it faced all these problems to a greater extent than before. Heresy was not limited to the erstwhile Other as it now crept into the ambitions of various sects previously within the confines of the thought and life of the Self. The relationship between the Shaiva and Vaishnava sects in the context of yet another stream— that of the Shaktas—would be worth investigating from this perspective. To what degree was there a rivalry among them? Or were there mutual adjustments? Were they linked to a potential following? The term *pashanda* initially applied to any sect now shifted in meaning and began to refer specifically to those sects that were being condemned as fraudulent by the more conservative. The point at which a religion recognizes that it has orthodoxy is often also the moment when a heterodoxy opposing it becomes apparent.

The emergence of these renouncers took on the characteristics of what may be called a counter-culture, at least to begin with. It was an entirely new kind of Other. It should not be confused with the ascetic with which it often is. The renouncer may have had traces of the ascetic but was actually quite distinct.

The one who wished to become an ascetic, the *samnyasi*, performed the funerary rituals that would have been required for him. He cut his ties with family and society, and went to live in isolation. Sometimes he would visit an *ashrama* in some distant place where other ascetics were living but essentially he was supposed to live away from others. This idea has of course disappeared from the many institutions that call themselves *ashramas* today and are anything but socially isolated. The ascetic's purpose was to search for ways to liberate his soul from rebirth. On his death he was not to be cremated but to be buried in a sitting position.

The renouncer, by joining an Order or a sect, renounced his prior social identity and assumed a new one as a member of that Order or sect. Family ties were not entirely discontinued. He did not regard himself as severed from society as the sects accepted patronage from virtually anyone who gave it, and worked towards acquiring a large lay following of people by convincing them of the teaching of the founders—at least of that version of the teaching which was being propagated by the particular sect he belonged to. The teaching was not conversion to a new religion but was intended more to give people a new ethical ideal. The Shramanas emphasized the centrality of improving the social good.

Renunciation is not a necessary component of dissent, but where it exists there is some element of dissent. To consider the views of the latter as we know does make for a greater representation of diverse opinion. Using this experience of the past and questioning the activities of the present can help define a better future. This, after all, was part of the purpose in imagining and projecting the future in the form of a millennial utopia, to be ushered in by the Buddha to come, the Buddha Maitreya.

The Shramana tradition recognized the difference in status given by society to men and to women. It did concede giving the choice of renunciation to women and quite a few took it. They had to get the consent of their husbands if they were married. Even women who were not from elite groups could make donations to the Buddhist Sangha and their donations were recorded. But it was not a choice that allowed autonomy to women since nuns were to be essentially subservient to the orders and the teaching of the monks. It did however assist in persuading women to become lay followers. Respect for nuns was not universal. According to one *dharma-shastra*, respectable women should have no communication with nuns. The *Arthashastra* states repeatedly that Buddhist and Jaina nuns can be employed as spies by the royal court. One wonders whether it was actually so or whether this was said to cast suspicion on the nuns.

Since they had a commitment to the welfare of society, the monks remained connected with the lay following. Unlike the *ashramas*—the forest hermitages of earlier times—these monasteries located near villages and towns were the institutional spine of the Buddhist and Jaina religions and, as such, had a marked presence in society. Their effective interventions may have encouraged other religious sects to establish similar institutions. When *brahmanas* received land grants of *agraharas* and when they established their *mathas*, there was a striking increase in their presence in the more fertile and wealthier parts of kingdoms. The same pattern can be noticed, not surprisingly, with the coming of the Sufis and their founding *khanqahs* and *dargahs* in the agriculturally and commercially richer areas, where patronage was forthcoming. For instance, there was much Sufi activity in the Multan region of southern Punjab and in the upper Doab with the arrival of the first Sufis. Important trade routes ran through this area and irrigation systems were introduced.

The institution encapsulating the teaching became the focus. A range of religious sects adopted this institutional form as they do to this day. Monasteries were locations for the study of religious and philosophical ideas and for meditation but many, in the course of just being present in the proximity of villages and towns, extended their concerns to matters political and social, expanding their range of Otherness. Their extension into taking on the function of social institutions imbued them with the power and authority that they required to formulate the codes by which communities would search for an identity. In this situation, dissent might still have had a religious form but in effect it began to relate to a greater degree to social concerns.

Their becoming wealthy and well established coincided with orthodoxies arising in these institutions and this, in turn, opened up some of them to further dissenting opinion. Earlier dissenting groups were also subjected to new concepts of disagreement and the pattern that emerged demonstrated the potential of being the Other. What was open to negotiation, depending on the focus of dissent, was the question of whether the dissent was helping to strengthen orthodoxy or was encouraging heterodoxy. All Shramana sects were not necessarily centres of dissent since there were debates within the overall thinking of their views. Similarly, there were disagreements among sects following other religious ideas. Dissent therefore has to be seen in relation to who is the particular Self.

Not all renouncers joined institutions and communities. There were individual renouncers who moved across the historical landscape in diverse forms, such as the *sadhu*, *faqir*, *jogi*, and were recognized as part of the larger category of the Other—but in their individual capacity. The renouncer opting out of society to work for the good of all gave him a status, and he acquired moral authority within society. This seems somewhat contradictory but it gave legitimacy to his dissent and to the social ethics that he taught, dissenting as he was from the views of the dominant groups. If he attracted supporters, then this in turn gave him a social leverage. Was this perhaps the reason why Kautilya, supporting authoritarian rule, discourages the state from allowing renouncers to enter newly settled lands? Presumably, the argument would be that if the state wishes to exercise complete power, it should disallow dissenting views—familiar from many histories of the past and the present. Where the state controlled the varied aspects of society as was advocated in the *Arthashastra*, this dictatorial authority gave it the power to disallow dissenting views.

We have to keep in mind that not all 'holy men' have arrived at renunciation or semi-renunciation after a serious understanding of why they have done so. Some adopt the symbols associated with holiness as individuals only to exploit them for personal advantage. There is something of a gamble in knowing how far the concern is real. Renunciation can be a genuine act of faith or it can be a disguise for exploiting the faith of others; hence the need to check the authenticity of the claims. There also has to be a balance of emphasis on the message or on the religious symbols and idioms. If the message is too heavily encumbered by the latter, it loses its force.

The period between the Mauryan and Gupta times was one of some competition for superiority, even if indirectly among sects. Hovering over the statements on political activities in the Manu *Dharmashastra* and the Kautilya *Arthashastra* is the fear of anarchy. A condition of anarchy is described as *matsyanyaya*, when the big fish eat the little fish. The texts speak of pervading evil and the wicked not being punished, without defining exactly who is meant by these references. Nevertheless, it is interesting that it is the activities of the big fish that crystallize the sense of anarchy.

Yet, in periods of emergency, Kautilya permits the king to confiscate the wealth of a religious institution. Later historical examples of this are described in detail in Kalhana's *Rajatarangini*, where we are told that towards the end of the first millennium AD various rulers of Kashmir used the excuse of a fiscal crisis to loot temples, culminating in the horrendous attacks on temples by the eleventh-century ruler Harshadeva.

Curiously, despite all these changes and challenges to existing norms, there seems to have been some hesitation in dissent turning into revolt. Dissent was perhaps a way of containing it. The awareness of the possibility of revolt was known but discouraged. Caste rules could be quietly reformulated as long as no questions were asked, or people could get way with it; new deities and rituals were incorporated into the formal religions, and occasionally new teaching hinting at a different kind of society could be spoken of among some people. This has been an ongoing process through the centuries—and explains the acceptance of interpolations into texts such as the *Mahabharata, Ramayana* and *Gita*. Through these interpolations, the texts were, as it were, living with the times.

The migration of discontented peasants from one kingdom to another is referred to, although it is disapproved of by the rulers since it resulted in a loss of revenue. As it has been argued, if peasants migrate, then it can be understood that they are agitating against an oppressive authority. But the right of subjects to revolt is not easily conceded in the texts of the earlier period. The *Mahabharata* allows the assassination of oppressive kings but only by those capable of making such a judgement such as the *brahmanas*. Buddhist sources, though, are more flexible.

This flexibility may be an outcome of the Buddhist view on the origin of the state, repeated in the *Mahabharata*. It is narrated that when the pristine utopia of human society began to decline with the introduction of kinship rules and ownership of property determining social behaviour, the people affected by this change gathered and elected one from among themselves to make laws and to rule over them in accordance with the laws. This notion of what can almost be called a social contract is consistent in Buddhist writing. In the texts authored by *brahmanas*, this comes at a later stage, the earlier argument favouring the raja being appointed by a deity.

References to peasants threatening to revolt appear to be made more frequently in the second millennium AD, but these may just have been rhetorical. Actual disturbances are few. Similarly, when some urban artisans also objected to the amount of taxes and rents they had to pay, an agreement was negotiated.

*

3. *Otherness Imprinted*

At this point I would like to pause and say that Otherness is not always the articulation arising from a person or a group reacting to a Self. It is not always a self-declaration. One group can impose it on another; a Self can impose it on a group to create an Other. This is done either to socially exclude the group upon whom the exclusion is imposed, or to convert the exclusion into social subordination. Many societies impose exclusion on certain sections largely in order to keep them subservient. Particular occupational groups are segregated and often these are groups that provide the material foundations on which the system functions, such as essential labour. One method of subjugating them is to make them unfree, to declare them as having no freedom or rights. Civilizations were built on the labour of slaves and serfs. What is taken as the creative period of Indian civilization coincides with references to various kinds of *avarnas*. This is a social Otherness, but it is not an Otherness that necessarily originates in dissent. Those excluded have no choice. Nevertheless, its presence has to be noticed since it can become the Otherness of dissent and protest, as has happened in various societies in recent times.

Renouncers voluntarily joined the alternative society that gave them a different identity. But this imposed Otherness—a major category—that we have frequently ignored, is a contrast to the ones I have mentioned earlier since it is an imposed and deliberate Otherness, an enforced social distancing to reiterate downgrading. The categories of the *avarna* are the lowest among castes if treated as castes, and consist of those outside the *varna* categories of caste, the lower castes, the untouchables and the *adivasis,* the latter living segregated in the forests. This Otherness was the creation of the uppermost caste, supported by those higher up in the hierarchy.

Some communities with their own identity were segregated to facilitate the use of their labour, such as the Chandalas who spoke their own language and observed their own social laws. The Chandala is known and ranked among the lowest in society. The *Gita* threatens that if a person disobeys established social observances, he can be reborn as either a dog or a pig or a Chandala. There is one intriguing story in the *Mahabharata* in a later section of the text, the inclusion of which remains puzzling. During a period of intense famine, the *brahmana* sage Vishwamitra was searching for food. He came to a Chandala village and saw a dead dog hanging in a hut and was about to eat it when the Chandala chastised him and reminded him of his *brahmana*-hood and purity, and the fact that if he ate the dog he would lose whatever merit he had accumulated. Nevertheless, the sage ate the dog and then proceeded to make up for the lost merit. It is a curious story. Such a situation would be unthinkable in the *dharma-shastras,* since his action would have demoted the sage from being a *brahmana.* One wonders why it was introduced into the *Mahabharata* and left without a detailed comment.

There was an insistence that the human being categorized as untouchable was so impure in body and mind that a person of caste would be polluted if he or she should even touch such a person. It is thought that this became most stringent when dissenting views among the upper castes had begun to proliferate in the first millennium AD. This aspect of social history was often set aside when describing the society of the 'golden age'.

There has been some discussion on why such a category had to be created. Some have argued that it had to do with converting the cow into a sacred animal. Those that removed the carcasses of dead cows and ate the flesh became the impure ones and were excluded. This may be a partial explanation, but for a social change of such magnitude, it required more than the eating of beef as the reason for exclusion. The other argument that these were in origin people who belonged to tribes that were subdued, then broken up and put to occupations considered degrading is a more plausible explanation. Who did the subduing, in what way and how they were forced into degrading occupations would, however, still need explaining.

The creation of such a subservient category ensured a permanent supply of bonded labour, as well as people who could thereby be forced to do the work that the rest of society was unwilling to do, categorizing it as degraded. The imposition was so oppressive that it disallowed opposition from those subordinated. It ensured an unchanging continuity through the permanent impoverishment of most among them. The distancing was reinforced by the assertion that the *avarna* included a category of inherently polluted people. To emphasize and legitimize the imposition, it was maintained that the pollution and hence impurity of this category was the counterweight, as it were, to the purity of the highest caste, that of the *brahmana*. The supposed purity of the *brahmana* and certain upper castes was balanced against the impurity imposed on the *asprishya* / untouchables. It was not accidental that many of the landowners at this time were *brahmana* recipients of grants of land and that the higher offices of governance were held by the upper castes. To secure their subjection, the *avarnas* were diminished in human terms and denied access to temples as sacred spaces. We have yet to investigate the religion of the *avarnas* in early times.

This Other did not have its origin in dissent. It had neither the right nor the opportunity to dissent. Yet some *avarnas* did dissent in their teaching as Bhakti *sants*. They were unable to alter social observances but they had a presence that was recognized, even if they came from castes ranked at the lowest level. Their teaching became a strong oral tradition. The later mythology in which their hagiographies are enveloped emphasizes three aspects: their devotion to the deity, abstract or otherwise, is reciprocated by the love that the deity has for the particular teacher; the *brahmanas* are hostile to the *sant* but are required to withdraw their hostility; and they sometimes receive effective patronage from royal women. The last is doubtless a subtle indication of a similar presence of the other group that lacks freedom—namely, the women. All three aspects reflect the anguish and the reality of the social norms that formed the context to the teaching of these *sants*.

Sometimes there is an inverted contestation. In the case of Ravidas, for instance, arguably the *avarna sant* with the largest following in our times, his hagiography states that he was a *brahmana* in his previous birth and an icon-worshipping disciple of Ramananda, but that he happened to eat meat and was therefore punished by being reborn in a low caste. This would seem to be an attempt to give him a high-status origin without denying his actual status. *Brahmana* authors of biographies of *sants* sometimes downplay conflict between the two and give upper-caste origins to these *sants,* albeit in a previous birth. Ravidas himself does not say that he is a follower of Ramananda.

In current times, the right to dissent comes with a little more force—at least in theory. The question is: What form will the dissent take? Attempts are being made to elide Dalit groups into the Hindu fold, but here caste comes in the way as it has done with conversions to non-Hindu religions as well. The emancipation from caste that is ultimately inevitable has to be with reference to all categories of castes. With the *avarna*, its effectiveness will come as a movement from within its own communities. This would be yet one more process of creating the Other. As regards the existing *avarna*, we have to ask who is creating it, for what purpose, and who is being forced to conform to it and why it continues. Those that have Otherness imposed on them in this manner have to resist it by questioning the legitimacy of the imposition.

The same holds true for what were called *atavikas* and *adivasis*, whom we now refer to as the Scheduled Tribes. These were the various peoples of relatively egalitarian communities identified by clans and clusters of clans who were essentially forest dwellers. As long as the forests were not encroached upon, they led their independent lives and were treated as culturally alien and distant by the villagers settled in areas that had been cleared of forests and were under cultivation. But with the expansion of the agrarian economy and deforestation, these communities were either pushed back further into the interior or else subordinated. Some among the latter were absorbed into the culture of the lower castes; others came to be treated as untouchable. Why and how this choice was made needs further investigation.

In the few cases where the *adivasi* clans had assisted adventurers to acquire political power, the new successful rulers made some concessions of status to them. At the coronation of certain Rajput rulers, the Bhil chief applied the *tilak*. An *adivasi* deity could be absorbed into the royal cult as might have happened with the Chandella adoption of the worship of Maniya Devi. The process by which such deities were adopted and adjusted to upper-caste worship can be seen in many instances across the subcontinent.

4. *The Bhakti* Sant *and the Sufi* Pir

My third example is a more complicated one. In the first instance, I referred to the individual—the *brahmana* who is the son of a *dasi*—from an alternative culture that had its disagreements with the established culture but who, in some instances, was believed to have supernatural powers that gave him enviable authority. His interaction was with a small group in the established society. The second instance was of a group of people, the Shramanas, who were essentially dissenting from Vedic Brahmanism, but subsequently an orthodoxy came about from within their own ranks; and although they continued to be dissenters in relation to the then-dominant society, some were conformists in their own society. Nevertheless, many of high status looked upon them as dissenting groups.

I shall now speak about the Other in the context of an even larger number of Others, and many Selves. I am going forward to yet another millennium and referring to the fifteenth to sixteenth centuries AD, a remarkable period of the Indian past, especially from the perspective of the history of religion and the interface of religion with society. There was, by now, an even greater social mixture. This is reflected in the teachings, the poems, the songs and the life of the time. Mughal Emperor Akbar was not just a flash in the pan creating new religious trends as some have suggested. There were many others like him. I shall be speaking of those far less exalted but whose activities as the Other went further.

My example is one facet of what has been called the Bhakti movement, a movement that arose in every part of the subcontinent under diverse persons described as *sants* / holy men. (It is preferable not to translate the word as 'saint', as is often done, since 'saint' is more commonly used for those that have a particular kind of status in Christian belief, a status which has different nuances from that of the Bhakti *sant*.) Initially, these were the Other in the context of existing religions. Going beyond the usual forms of worship, they expressed untrammelled devotion to a deity of their choice or to the abstract idea of deity. It was a departure from both Puranic Hinduism and Islam. Some arose from the ideas that shaped religious thought at that time in India; others from ideas that came with the Sufi schools that arrived from Central Asia and Persia and settled in India, forming yet more Others. These processes were crucial to breakaway sects. Given the interface of cultures, a spectacular efflorescence of a range of religious teaching followed, affecting many levels of society.

This shaped the practice and belief of those who, in modern times and largely for the sake of convenience, were brought together under the single uniform label of Hindu. It also shaped the belief of some of those who were at that time called Yavanas, Shakas and Turushkas, and for whom we today use the single uniform label of Muslim. These uniform labels distort the meaning of what religion meant in those times. How were they spoken of in their own times? What is of greater historical interest are the cross-beliefs coming from mixed origins with an appeal to those that did not conform strictly to any religion. Much of the practice of religion at this time came from such sources. In our rush to categorize all thought and activity into the binaries of formal religions—Hindu and Muslim for the second millennium AD—we have missed the larger world of nuances, ambiguities and subtleties so characteristic of much that happens in a society, and perhaps more so in the societies of the past. This was different from the earlier period when, despite the binary, the religious identity was more often that of the sect.

The Bhakti movement, or what has been called Devotional Hinduism, was in some ways a part of Puranic Hinduism yet in some ways apart (if I may be forgiven the pun). Its earlier teachers were Vaishnava and Shaiva preachers, poets and singers of the peninsula; from the second millennium AD, it found voices in the north. It did not require the appurtenances of Puranic Hinduism, and although it worshipped the same or similar gods, it was in a sense a bifurcation from the former. Further, there was within it a separation between the *sants* of the lower castes not altogether averse to being virtually *nastikas*, and others who were devotees usually of one of the Puranic deities. This distinction has been attempted in the separation of *nirguna* and *saguna bhakti*, devotion to an abstract or to a manifest notion of deity, but the differences speak to much more. Devotion was not always linked to temples, priests and rituals even where the worship was of an established deity.

Again, there were two streams articulating *dharma* that were not identical. One, *brahmana*-dominated temple-based religion that commanded wealth, intervened in political and social matters and claimed primacy as a religion. The other consisted of the multiple religious articulations supported, to a larger extent, by the middle castes and the *avarnas*, or the occasional *brahmana*, and whose belief and worship, even when dedicated to a Puranic god, varied from that of the first group. This latter group expressed itself through a large range of sects identified either by the central deity—such as the Alvars and Nayanars of the south—or by a person who founded a sect, such as Chaitanya, or indeed by yet another category, such as Kabir, Dadu, Ravidas, Chokhamela, Nanak, who focused on the abstract idea of deity. This difference may have been in part due to the social identities of the *sants* that led them away from the conventional form of worship. The latter group hints at the continuation of some ideas earlier associated with the Shramanas, albeit in new forms.

Neither the Bhakti *sants* nor the Sufi *pirs* were founding new religions. They were trying to liberate religion from what they saw as orthodoxies and jaded conventions enforced by those who had a powerful status and authority over formal religions. Significantly, the teaching of these many Others was open to any person. Their Otherness may have varied according to whom they were addressing as the Self. Politically, those rulers that had the blessings of the more revered *pirs* could claim a further legitimacy to rule. This is reminiscent of

the earlier custom where *brahmanas* constructed appropriate genealogies for *maharajas*.

Whatever the previous religious identity of their followers may have been, it was largely irrelevant to the
sants and the *pirs*. Nor did they endorse caste conventions. On both counts they were dissenters. The *sants*
made it a point to use the language of the people so that
their teachings could be widely understood. The deity
worshipped could be in the form of an abstract idea or
an icon. Kabir referred to the abstract idea of God, as
did Nanak in his reference to Rab, an Arabic name for
God used extensively in the Panjabi language by people
of every religion. Some who worshipped Krishna as the
incarnation of Vishnu, often as an icon, also sang of him
as a person who had been in their midst. The teaching
was informal—hymns of adulation and devotion—as
also were the scant rituals.

Among the earlier *sants* were Kabir, Ravidas, Dadu
and Chokhamela, for whom the identity of deity was not
the pivot of their teaching. They were of the lower castes
and were searching for their utopias. Kabir, a strikingly
unusual thinker, explored the world of open belief. To
that extent, there is an echo of the earlier Shramanic tradition, but no obvious connection. Ravidas had a vision
of a city of the future that was devoid of social inequality
and therefore registered an absence of sorrow, and hence
was called Be-gam-pura / the city without sorrow. It is
significant that the coming of the millennium, as it were,
for the *avarna* was not Judgement Day as among the

Abrahamic religions, or the catastrophic end of the universe at the end of the Kaliyuga as among the Hindus—salvaged perhaps by the coming of Kalkin. It was akin to the Buddhist idea of the coming of Buddha Maitreya who would bring the return of the Buddhist utopia of a just society and the prevalence of *dhamma*. It was the quality of the society and the prevalence of social justice that was paramount. These *sants* saw themselves not as a single Other but as diverse Others, even though linked by the message of devotion.

The diversity is evident, for example, in a different approach to the act of *bhakti* / devotion, as in the verses of Lal Ded in Kashmir and Nanak in Punjab. Lal Ded was a Shiva *bhakt*, yet this did not stop her inspiring the Sufi poet of Kashmir, Sheikh Nuruddin, popularly known as Nand *rishi*. Nanak's verses drew from Sufi teachings, most famously those of Baba Farid as well as Kabir, Ravidas and some others, all of whom he quotes. These exchanges, borrowings and internalizations deeply enriched the thought of the times, hinting at the answers to current questions. There was perhaps also a wish to give a location and a touch of historicity to those being posited as worthy of worship. The biography of Rama was traced in the topography of Ayodhya and recorded in the *Ayodhya-mahatmya*, and the landscape of Vrindavana and its neighbourhood was associated with events in Krishna's life. This was to coincide with these locations becoming sites of pilgrimage, a change that brings much pleasure to those who can worship through making a pilgrimage and much wealth for those advocating the pilgrimage.

Then came the cloudburst that immersed so many. This was the immense popularity of Krishna *bhakti* projected through devotion to Krishna and to the worship of Krishna and Radha. Krishna Vasudeva had been central to many Vaishnava sects. Two major texts gave it added status: the *Bhagavata Purana,* which in the tradition of Puranic texts dedicated to a deity—in this case Vishnu—had much on the worship of Krishna; and literary compositions such as Jayadeva's *Gita-Govinda,* exalting the love of Krishna and Radha, which has been interpreted by some as symbolic of the love and devotion of the worshipper for the deity. The form it took, even if symbolic, contradicted the conventions of the *dharma-shastra* social code. The impulse remained intensive with devotion as the act of worship. Krishna *bhakti* became the focus of another set of Bhakti *sants*, speaking from places near and far, as, for instance, Chaitanya, Eknath, Surdas and Meera, among others. That it was one of the cultural idioms of the sixteenth century gives it other meanings.

Those who were expressing themselves in this new idiom of *bhakti* were articulating more than a love and devotion to a deity. It was significant that they were doing so in their individual capacity. Seemingly in keeping with recognized forms of worship, there was implicit in this an element of dissent. The *bhakt* followed a *sant* and worshipped a deity of his or her own choice. One is reminded of the renouncer who became that from personal choice, even if the object of worship was entirely different.

The centrality of Radha among the many sects that worshipped Krishna and Radha as a pair ensured that the presence of the woman was evident. This was not unknown since goddesses were present in the bigger pantheon. But the role of Radha was significantly different and had to do with the agency of worship drawing on love and devotion. The more effective goddesses often controlled power through violence and force. Radha was not from the same mould as Durga.

There were much-revered women *sants* such as Lal Ded and Mirabai—not to mention those in south India—whose dissent as women became a kind of double dissent. Socially they did not hide their independence of thought and action and this put more barriers in their path that they had to overcome. Their acceptance as teachers was not so smooth. That as women they were preaching and singing about *bhakti*, a new belief system, more openly being preached by men *sants* was in a sense dissent enough, but that they were asserting the fact of being women and doing so effectively took some accepting. When Mirabai, coming from the Rajput upper caste, refused to acknowledge her husband because of her devotion to the deity, it was regarded with intense disapproval to the point where she went into self-imposed exile. Her statements and actions encouraged her rejection by her social circle. But her hymns became popular as they expressed the anguish of the subordinated—women and lower castes—and she became their voice.

These *sants* were joined by other worshippers and poet-singers emerging from a variety of religious and social backgrounds, whom we rarely mention these days when speaking of Bhakti, whether as a religious or a social articulation. Disciples initially of other religious persuasions clustered around the *sants*. Among them were Ras Khan from a wealthy zamindar family, and Abdul Rahim Khan-i-Khanan who held high offices in the Mughal administration. Haridas was the name taken by an important Yavana disciple of Chaitanya, known popularly as Jaban Haridas, where Jaban is the Bengali for Yavana. Sufi poets even of a slightly later period, such as Bulleh Shah, Malik Muhammad Jayasi and Sayyad Mubarak Ali Bilgrami, to mention just a few, wrote exquisite poems in adoration of Krishna to express their *bhakti* / devotion. The focus on love would have drawn many with Sufi interests. These compositions continue to be sung as verses in Hindustani classical music and as accompaniments to dance, and on various festive occasions. Inevitably it was said of them that these Yavanas were attaining *moksha* through this *bhakti*.

What I am saying is nothing new. It is well known to those familiar with the history of these times as well as those who are familiar with its poetry and music—in fact, what may broadly be called a pervasive cultural stream of medieval North India. However, it seldom enters public discussion on Bhakti, partly because the

Otherness of Bhakti and the implicit dissent of many of its compositions are rarely referred to, the focus being on treating the compositions as essential to conventional worship in the more established religions. The question that has not been answered adequately is why there was such an upsurge of Krishna *bhakti* at this historical moment in North India, drawing in a variety of people from a range of what we today label as different formal religions. What led to these new forms of belief that crossed prior religions, geographical boundaries, castes, languages? What encouraged this form of dissent—for dissent it was initially? What did it signify?

An obvious question is: Why did highly placed Muslims, and not inconsequential ones at that, turn their creativity towards Krishna *bhakti*? Modern historians have called them Muslim Vaishnavas, but they did not call themselves that. They called themselves Krishna *bhaktas*. Their intention pointed to their identity and possibly reflected far more than religious devotion. It was a cultural indicator of a substantial kind, yet we hardly give it attention. This can be partly explained by the narrowness of the contemporary definition of Indian culture that excludes those aspects that bring in the wider assenting and dissenting dimensions that are inevitable in the creation of any expansive culture.

We often forget that cultures evolve from the interface of many strands in the life of communities and reflect a mixture of many patterns. No culture is singular in its origins. Culture assumes a form once the strands are well integrated. We overlook the fact that the Mughal–Rajput alliances had many dimensions apart from the overtly political. For instance, the Kacchwaha Rajputs of Amber claiming high status as Suryavamsha *kshatriyas* gave their daughters to the Mughal ruling family who were thought of as Turushkas. This contributed to a Rajput presence and practices in the Mughal royal family. These would have been viewed by the Muslim orthodoxy as acts of defiance by the non-Muslim, and on other grounds disapproved of by orthodox *brahmanas*.

The patronage of the Govind Dev temple at Vrindavan with its unusual Indo-Persian architecture strikingly different from the other enormous temples constructed in this period reflected the mixture of Rajput and Mughal. This joint patronage doubtless helped to enliven Vrindavan as the focus of Krishna *bhakti*. This was more than a matter of marriage alliances. It was also making a statement about finding a new identity, giving it form and imbuing it with legitimacy, not to mention its political ramifications. Where Krishna *bhakti* is linked to the patronage of the Kacchwaha and the Mughals, there it touches the political culture of both and its activities acquire yet another dimension. Does dissent gradually give way to accommodation when the latter is thought to be politically more expedient?

Puranic Hinduism was now at one level inducting some local dimensions of *bhakti* and therefore incorporating regional cults that sometimes became sects at other levels. Examples of this could be Jagannath in

Odisha, said to have had beginnings in tribal worship in the area; Vitthala in Maharashtra, thought to have grown out of the worship of a hero-stone; Hinglaj-mata in Sind, which has been and is of special importance to nomadic pastoralists and traders; Bonbibi the forest goddess in the Sundarbans, and so on. Some were stitched into Puranic Hinduism; others had an identity as juxtaposed sects. That they were local cults is evident from their followers being in the main from particular regions, and the cult itself being less known in other regions. Earlier cult figures such as Krishna and Rama had a wider appeal and prominence when the literary and religious discourse was opened up to larger audiences. They attracted a diversity of followers and this inevitably resulted in multiple versions of the narratives. This gave a local flavour to the local version and yet the narrative linked the local version to a wider region. Sometimes the local version made a statement that differed from the established text.

To turn to another situation of those times, namely, the view that the Muslim was always the Other and qualified by his religion—Islam. Even a preliminary look at the sources indicates that within the structures of Indian society at the time, that which can be labelled as consent or dissent, accommodation or confrontation, are far more complicated matters than we have assumed. This is not a new feature but existed among well-defined communities as we have seen from earlier history. What is important is to recognize the transition towards consent or dissent of varying degree, and to ask what determines the direction.

We use the label of Muslim uniformly today for anything with a touch of Islam. It was used only occasionally in public discourse and then too with particular reference in earlier centuries. What we often overlook is that non-Muslims did not generally refer to Muslims by the single label of Muslim as we do today. In those days, references to them in Sanskrit and other languages were based on a different category of names such as Yavanas or Shakas or Turushkas. These labels were ethnic and not religious. They also link up interestingly with earlier history. Yavana was used for the Greeks and those who came from the West. So it was used for the Arabs and later for anyone regarded as foreign coming from the West, such as even Queen Victoria. The ancient Shakas were the Scythians from Central Asia, the homeland also of the Turushkas, the Turks. So strong was the association of the Turushkas with Central Asia that Kalhana, writing in the eleventh century in his *Rajatarangini,* describes the Kushans coming from Central Asia in the early first millennium AD as Turushkas. These, therefore, were historically authentic names used for the Arabs, Afghans, Turks and Mughals who came from these regions. It also suggests that they were viewed as descended from the earlier peoples as indeed some historically were. The labels of Hindu and Muslim as referring to those identified by uniform monolithic religions came later.

However, some Turushkas on occasion are also referred to in Sanskrit sources as *mlecchas,* used either in a derogatory sense or as just a passing reference to difference. For example, in one Kakatiya inscription from the Deccan, in Sanskrit and Telugu, the Delhi Sultan Muhammad bin Tughlaq, after a successful campaign in the area, is described by the local defeated raja as a dreadful man who killed *brahmanas,* destroyed temples, looted farmers, confiscated the land granted to *brahmanas,* drank wine and ate beef. This was now to become the stereotypical description of a Muslim ruler whenever a negative projection was required. It carries an echo of the description of the *kala* Yavanas / black Yavanas of a millennium earlier in the *Yuga Purana,* when probably the Indo-Greeks were being referred to in an uncomplimentary manner. Some Yavanas patronized Buddhism and this may have been the cause for complaint. In the eighteenth century, the same description is applied to the Marathas. The Bengali *Maharashtra Purana* refers to Maratha raiders as killers of cows and *brahmanas*—a phrase that it seems was sometimes used in unlikely situations merely to express strong antagonism.

But to return to the Tughlaqs—inscriptions from elsewhere make a different assessment of the same man. A Sanskrit inscription from the vicinity of Delhi issued by a Hindu merchant during the reign of Muhammad bin Tughlaq is full of praise for the Tughlaq rulers, describing them as the historical successors to the Tomar and Chauhan Rajputs with just a passing reference to one of them as *mleccha*. Obviously, here it is meant as being different in language and is not used in a derogatory sense, since the Tughlaq rulers are applauded in the same inscription; and in any case who would dare to use a term of contempt for the sultan?

These identities, however, are not without their own occasional fears. The thirteenth-century *Brihaddharma Purana*, for example, has a major worry that the Yavanas will destroy the code of *varna-ashrama-dharma* on which rests the ideological edifice of the Brahmanical view of caste society, and will introduce their own gods, texts and teaching to replace what exists. From the Brahmanical perspective, the continuance of *varna* society was crucial.

What complicates the Otherness of these communities is precisely that they cannot all be put into one bracket. They also had many Selves. An early category of Yavanas would have been the Arabs who were trading with coastal India even prior to the rise of Islam. They continued this trade into later times as traders who were now Muslim. They settled on both eastern and western coasts of the peninsula. Inscriptions record these settlements and their participation in local life. This latter took the form of intermarrying locally, and in some cases, as under the Rashtrakutas, holding high office in local administration. In one case, an Arab governor of a district in western India ordered the grant of land to a *brahmana* grantee on behalf of the Rashtrakuta ruler.

Inevitably, these settlements became the focal points of new kinship arrangements and religious sects as well as occupations. These reflected the observance of custom as a mixture of Islamic belief and practice with that of various local Hindu and Jaina sects. Thus there emerged the Bohras and the Khojas in western India, the Navayaths further south and the Mapillas in Kerala, as well as others in Bengal. Given the trade across the Arabian Sea, there were communities of Bohras and Khojas in West Asia as well, for example, at Yemen, and in East Africa. To the extent that these sects evolved from a range of existing religious beliefs and practices, they expressed their individuality in the differentiation they made among themselves and in their proximity or distance from existing religions. They were initially groups that stood apart, geared to their particular occupational preferences that introduced cultural elements from many sources. Were they expressing dissent from the established religions where they distanced themselves?

What gives another dimension to this particular Otherness is not only its own origins but also that it has many Selves. We may well ask whether every Muslim was viewed as a *mleccha* by upper-caste Hindus in the areas where such communities were established? This was not so for a number of obvious reasons. There were differences among the various communities of Arab origin settled in coastal areas and reflecting the societies amid which they settled and with whom they intermarried, and they did not see others like themselves as identical despite their Islamic component. Local cultural identities made their own marks in various ways. The Bohras of Gujarat, for example, would have differentiated themselves from the Mapillas of Kerala. Were such communities regarded as dissenters and un-Islamic by orthodox Islam or were they acceptable?

Some of the most important official positions in the Sultanate and Mughal administration were held by the upper castes, by Rajputs, *brahmanas* and *kayasthas*, and by the Jainas. The first group had status in the existing society and the latter had also held high office. The *kayasthas* had traditionally been in charge of the administration in many kingdoms, and the Jainas were regarded as particularly proficient in commerce and finance. The social distance would presumably have also depended on caste, hence the upper castes at the court. Local administration would in the main have been in the hands of the local gentry with some overseers that were officially appointed. That in caste terms the rulers they served were technically *mleccha* does not seem to have been a problem, or else it was set aside. And as to who was dissenting from whom, that becomes a moot problem.

It is likely that those lower down the social scale would have mixed even more easily on all sides, dependent both on the requirements of occupations and on the flexibility of religion. Religious festivals were occasions that went beyond just an occupational interdependence and were observed jointly, as also the worship of local-level *sants* and *pirs*. Dissent then becomes far more complex than merely the need for a change of religion. Are social perceptions problematic even if given a religious glaze?

The social distancing of the *savarna* and the *avarna* communities was immutable and continued even among those who had converted to Islam or those who had become Sikhs. Theoretically, these religions did not observe caste distinctions, but in effect there was a distancing between erstwhile upper and lower castes. The exclusion of Dalits continued as conversion did not liberate them from caste. The lowest castes may have been equal to the upper castes in the eyes of Allah, but not in the eyes of the existing upper castes, irrespective of the religion they followed. There is a social message of dissent from the formal social codes in the teachings of the *bhaktas* from the lower castes and *avarnas*, which we should listen to.

The Krishna *bhaktas* who were born Muslim were viewed as the Other by two categories of Selves. The *qazis* and *mullahs* of orthodox Islam strongly disapproved of them as did orthodox *brahmanas*. On occasion, the *qazi* tried to win back the *bhakta* by resorting to negotiation but this rarely succeeded. It continued until it became helpful to the formal religions to incorporate some of these teachings. Therefore, both the Other and the Self have to be carefully defined each time either is referred to in different historical contexts. This might be a necessary exercise in clarifying identities, and more so where there is an overlap.

An interesting comment on this situation comes from a sixteenth-century Sanskrit text, the *Prasthana-bheda* of the highly respected philosopher Madhusudana Sarasvati. It is an account of the current philosophical schools. Insofar as it comments on religion, it is apparent that the sects do not all conform to a monolithic Hinduism. In fact, he makes a separate mention of those that do not, such as the Buddhists, Jainas, Charvakas, and he also mentions the Turushkas. Is it evident from what he says that he is defining himself not as a Hindu but as a *brahmana*? For him one of the big divisions in philosophical and religious thought is based on the Vedic and non-Vedic differences. He uses the early definitions of the *astika : nastika* kind. He clubs the Buddhist, Jaina and Charvaka sects as being non-Vedic and, in this context, also refers to the teachings of the Turushkas (the Muslims as we would call them today) as being similar. And why? Because they were all *nastika* / non-believers.

For the Charvakas, Jainas and Buddhists, this is a repetition of what was said of them by *brahmana* authors many centuries earlier. The Shramanas were Buddhists and Jainas and had been spoken of with hostility in some Sanskrit compositions of upper-caste authors. In a few Sanskrit plays, the entry of a Jaina monk is regarded as an ill omen. To these three, Madhusudana Sarasvati adds the fourth, the Turushkas. Whereas the earlier three did not believe in any deity, and therefore were rightly called non-believers, the Turushkas, however, did believe in a deity, because they believed in Allah. But since Allah was not of the Vedic or Puranic pantheon, he was unacceptable, so they too were *nastika*. Interestingly, the author also brackets all four of them together as *mleccha*. The *bhaktas* presumably are not excluded at least not those of them that worship the Puranic deities although they say little or nothing about the Vedic deities.

What is beginning to receive some attention although long overdue is the interaction between the Bhakti and Sufi teachers. Their emphasis on devotion as a form of worship brought them together as did the emphasis on love for the abstract deity. But there were of course differences in how these were projected. Some among them had a message of dissent; others did not or did to a lesser degree. Some attempted to set up monastic orders or organizations parallel to monastic orders, as this was useful in providing an institutional base, which in turn can speak to authority more cogently than individual followers. Where property comes to be involved, the question of inheritance becomes primary. The supporters of each fanned out and again there rose a range of sects, some reasonably close in thought and practice and some quite distant.

Religions emerge and evolve in the context of existing beliefs and practices. These can be formulated into a kind of discipline or can remain free-floating ideas. New religious ideas in such situations tend to be eclectic. This can be observed of the sects of the second millennium AD. One hesitates to use the term 'influence' as it is often misunderstood as the domination of one over the other, and the term 'syncretic' hints at a binary. But the freedom to choose that was characteristic of the Bhakti *sants* is in essence eclectic. Needless to say, the historical context that provides the proximity of varying beliefs has also to be considered. The act of being eclectic assumes that there were distinctive, recognizable elements that were consciously chosen to define and identify the new religious articulations. The debate as to whether a sect belonged to a particular formal religion is not necessarily illuminating in terms of understanding the teaching of the sect, nor is it always called for. It is perhaps more to the point to understand what the teachers of the new sect made of the elements they chose from the existing spread, and what they invented.

Among the more evocative dialogues of these times were those between some of the Sufis and certain sects of Yogis/Jogis. Interestingly, both were the Others to the formal religions of Islam and Hinduism. One could ask whether or not the eclecticism of the Sufi sects coming from Central Asia could have been vaguely continuing the occasional idea of earlier times when various Buddhist sects were established in parts of Central Asia and were giving rise to eclectic versions of particular Buddhist ideas. This would be prior to the spread of Islam from the early second millennium. It is an intriguing thought that in both North India and Central Asia, Buddhism declined just prior to the coming of Islam. Were there any resonances?

In the broad expanse of relative free-thinking that characterizes those that live on the edges of society and claim to pursue the freedom to think of alternative ways of enhancing the social good and the quality of individual life, there were those that belonged to one sect but were in dialogue with others by way of exchanging ideas on these problems. Some of the dialogues had roots in what was being discussed among the sects both in India and just beyond the frontiers. The Nath Yogis, for instance, are known to have had conversations with various Sufi sects. An example of this was the avid interest of the sixteenth-century Gwalior-born Muhammad Ghawth, who belonged to the Shattari sect of Sufis, in the teaching of the Nath Yogis. He translated their Sanskrit text, the *Amritakunda*, into Persian. Was the interest in a text of the Nath Yogis a matter of intellectual curiosity alone or was this also an attempt to comprehend—in the process of translating the text—the thinking of those that nurtured some elements of dissent?

★

5. A Recapitulation

My discussion of dissent has so far been in the context of groups that have questioned aspects of what went into the making of the dominant religions of the Indian past, and more particularly the one most prominent. This has in turn contributed to some recognized forms taken by the religion, forms that have a bearing on its conservatism as well as its departures from orthodoxy. By insisting on the singular, the monolithic and the uniform, the argument is unnecessarily forced and leads to something of a closure. I would endorse the exploration of the diverse and the plural and the methods of dissent or accommodation or such like that are now beginning to be recognized in the history of the interaction of religions with societies. This is far more to the point when discussing the religions of India. It seems to me that the reformulations within these can be better observed and with insight if they are read through the sects that they generated and which represent their thoughts and activities. The relationship pattern of the Abrahamic religions to their societies sits uncomfortably in the Indian context. One obvious reason for this is the difference in the way the societies are structured.

I would like to argue that it is because of the absence of emphasizing the monolithic and the uniform in religion that dissent took the form that it did and, to some extent, continues to do. Confrontations did occur and some were violent as they still are. This is not surprising given the sharpness of social distinctions in Indian society. Nevertheless, it is because there is the possibility of juxtaposing the undercurrents of dissent and allowing them space that there is also flexibility in contention. This would require us to view Hinduism—the religion of the largest number—not as a single, continuous, unchanging institution but, rather, as a series of reformulated institutions of which some get amalgamated with what was there before and many that have a lively continuity as sects juxtaposed among a plurality of other such. The interface therefore of these sects with various communities and with each other would have patterns that differ from those projected as monolithic religions. Viewing religion in India only from the perspective of monolithic religions, coexisting or in conflict from time to time, as is more frequently done, could be misleading.

The term 'sect' refers to those that follow a particular way of thought and the membership is by choice. The terms generally used in early sources are *pashanda* and *sampradaya*. The first seems to have referred to any group that formalized itself as a sect. Emperor Ashoka's references to them are neutral in terms of disapproval or approval. But in later texts such as the *Puranas*, the word is used specifically for those regarded as heretics, teaching false doctrines, and on occasion for the Shramana sects too. It ceases to be a neutral term. *Sampradaya* has a relatively stable meaning and refers to those who join a group that claims an earlier tradition for its teaching— as many sects do—and assumes a continuity into the future.

It is not my intention to suggest that the only forms of dissent are those that arise in relation to religion. I have taken my examples from perceptions relating broadly to religion because these forms of dissent often had the more wide-ranging impact in the past and are the more obviously noticeable. They are also the ones that are more frequently written about in past times. They are not confined to changes in religious orientation since they also intervene in the institutions of society. The context of the examples I have discussed is familiar. The demonstration of dissent in such examples perhaps has greater clarity.

I would like to pause for a moment and recapitulate my view of the different phases of the dominant religion in India, by way of a background to what I shall be discussing in the final part of this essay. I would also like to reiterate the point that forms of dissent can and often do shape the reformulations of ideas pertaining to religious and social forms. My contention is that Hinduism underwent various reformulations in reacting and adjusting to significant historical changes, some segments of society being sensitive to the requirements of an altering historical context. Recognizing this makes it a more flexible religion and of greater verve than the rather confined form in which it is often projected. This view has been and is still battling the pressures from powerful Indian social and political groups to try and keep it within the defined colonial formula of its current influential reformulation.

We have not given attention to the historical reformulations of its history and their interface with Indian
society, nor recognized them sufficiently as adjustments
to historical change and to the challenge from dissenting
groups. These are adjustments that all belief systems
have to make the world over; some religions make them
more easily and obviously, some in a more intriguing
manner than others, and some problematically. They
affect in turn the forms of dissent that are opposed to
them. In making these distinctions, I am suggesting that
what we call Hinduism has been a religion that has
reacted closely to historical change, causing recognizable
alterations and mutations in both belief and in those that
identify with it. This is not specific to Hinduism and
could be said of all religions, but I think it is more pertinent to the range of diverse historical forms included
in what we call Hinduism.

To ignore the contribution of dissenting ideas to
these reformulations, or their failure to encourage the
necessary mutations, is to ignore the impressive presence of dissent in assessing the cultivation of religion in
India and in the underpinning of many social forms.
This I have tried to show in the three examples that I
have discussed. The examples relate to three crucial
categories of change pertinent to the historical narrative
of the religion.

A survey, however brief, of the history of religion as
conventionally understood pertaining to the subcontinent cannot begin at the beginning since we are as yet

unclear about the Harappan religion. Intelligent guesses derive from a reasoned analysis of the objects such as figurines, painted motifs on pottery, depictions of scenes and ideas on the seals often in association with pictograms. We have therefore to wait for a credible decipherment of the pictograms to provide reliable readings of what is being stated in them. Meanwhile, given all the uncertainty, there are any number of theories afloat. Some have argued that the continuity of the Harappan religion could well be found more in the substratum religions of post-Harappan times than in any dominant religion.

We may therefore take as the starting point the first and, for the moment at least, the well-defined religion whose texts are available. This was the Vedic religion— Vedic Brahmanism as it has been called. From the sources that we have, it appears to have evolved both in ritual and belief as the religion of one social category— that of the *brahmanas*, but in the context, nevertheless, of other less-defined religious beliefs and practices of which we have fewer details. The presence of the latter is evident, more indirectly perhaps than directly, as is now well known. My first example was an attempt to indicate the kind of differences that existed and the adjustments that can be made to avoid confrontation. What then were the cultural traits that might have seeped into the culture of what we regard as the Self from that of the Other?

Many of the deities of lesser importance in this first phase seem to surface in the second phase of Hinduism, symbolizing some differences with the first. The second phase has been called Puranic Hinduism, recorded in the *Puranas* and is a post-Vedic development. It registers differences apart from the prominent deities, in the forms of worship that change, as in the building of temples and the worship of icons, initially on a relatively smaller scale than the large-scale *yajnas*. Nevertheless obeisance continues to be paid to the *Vedas* although for the larger public it was a tenuous connection. This form was in competition with Shramanic religions and schools of thought—pre-eminently the Buddhist, and including the Jaina and Ajivika—that denied the basic tenets of Vedic Brahmanism, as also did the Charvaka.

The religious duality of Brahmanism and Shramanism was only too visible up to the mid- to late first millennium AD as demonstrated in my second example. Among the more important aspects that gave power and authority to Shramanism was the crucial role of its organization and the institutions it established. In the Buddhist case, this was the Sangha and the *vihara* / monastery. To this was added the fine-tuning of the act of receiving donations from wealthy sources. This possibly was a lesson to other religious groups, not all of whom understood it, although some understood it only too well. The fact that it was a dissenting group may have forced the Buddhists to think of using organization and institutions as hallmarks in their relationship with society. The quality of the structures that it built in the centuries just before and after the beginning of the Christian era are remarkable and contrary to the structures used by Vedic Brahmanism in their forms of worship. This was part of the dissent, the other part being of course the challenge to the belief of the religion being questioned. The denial of divinity was a major divide but this was to alter in later centuries. The *Brahmana–Shramana* duality took other forms in the succeeding millennium.

Brahmanic control in the second phase tends to be of a different kind, extending over the temple and the *matha* as the institutional bases of the religion, associated with Puranic Hinduism. At one level, it could be seen as the consolidation through the centuries of the Brahman-ical control over the religion of the upper castes—but in a new form. At another level, equally widespread and popular forms of the religion were the non-Brahmanic articulations of the *bhakti* movements where the deities were manifested in variant ways, the form of worship focused on devotion, and the institution of the temple was initially not the focus. Control included having to make some concessions to those that were less free in society—women and the lower castes. In some cases, the parallel forms eventually came together to some degree; in other cases, they remained apart.

Puranic Hinduism expressed its reverence for Vedic Brahmanism and incorporated the occasional deity and ritual. But the Vedic religion remained essentially the religion of the *brahmanas* and a few upper castes who patronized it. The patronage remained socially and eco-nomically effective and the recipients benefitted from this. The form taken by the religion in the first millennium AD had new features: the centrality of the two deities Vishnu and Shiva was focused on, the pantheon being gradually enlarged, especially when other cults were incorporated such as that of Shakta-Shakti; temples were first thought of and started to be built from the Gupta period and icons came to be worshipped more effectively than in previous times. This was a departure. The mythology went back to older sources and wove in earlier myths. The texts used for establishing this form—the *Puranas*—differed in form and content from the Vedic corpus. Much of the spread of this religion at the popular level was a successful interweaving of the Puranic religion with varieties of local deities and a large following from castes lower down the social scale. It is perhaps plausible to suggest that some ideas and institutions were quietly borrowed from the Shramanic religions. The interweaving in the later period in more distant areas and among the lower castes seems to have been a way of exercising control since the elite was dependent on their labour, craftsmen and technicians, as they in turn were dependent on the elite for providing employment.

Whereas the religion of the upper castes focused more on Puranic Hinduism, that of the lower castes had a more local and regional focus. The worship of trees, plants and animals goes back to earliest times, as probably do a number of *yakshi* cults and the *grama-devatas* / village deities. If longevity and continuous worship is a criterion of established religion, then these latter cults were probably more long-lasting than some of the textual varieties.

Speaking of local cults and their elevation, a fine illustration of the process of venerating local figures and deities and their being finally inducted into the Puranic religion comes from a significant religious articulation in Maharashtra. It is linked to the widespread prevalence of the cult of the hero given a particular orientation in this part of the country. It is sometimes linked to the worship of the *sati*, although the prevalence of this varies. Initially, large stones were erected to commemorate the heroes who had died defending the village, and frequently the cattle, or in a local battle. These were simple depictions of the hero with weapons and, occasionally, a horse.

Over the centuries, the memorial became increasingly elaborate, with some showing the scene of the death and the *apsaras* taking the hero to heaven, together with some symbols of his religious affiliation and a narrative of the event given in an inscription. Some of these stones were moved from the premises of the village and placed in the courtyard of the temple. Stones memorializing *satis* were largely symbolic, with a few distinctive set of symbols associated with sati-stones. In a few places in later periods, they were housed in a specially constructed temple.

The coming together of these multiple facets in the making of many cults that constituted Puranic Hinduism is demonstrated in the worship of Vishnu in his Vitthala / Vithoba form as in the main temple at Pandharpur in Maharashtra. Some have argued that his image in the sanctum has a stance identical with that of hero-stones of the region, suggesting an original link to the religion of pastoralists. The hero was he who protected their cattle. This would not be surprising in an area where a pastoral economy was prevalent. The hero-cum-Vitthala is now embedded in Vaishnava mythology, the more so when he became the prime deity of many Bhakti *sants* of the region, pre-eminently the much-revered Tukaram. This becomes the source of many avenues of perceiving the interaction between religious and social demands involved in this process. Up to a point, it is this gamut of social identities that goes into the making of a successful cult or a sect that also permits a greater articulation of dissent, should it be required.

Puranic Hinduism carried the bifurcation that I have referred to earlier. The temples, *mathas* and centres of learning remained under *brahmana* control, but the even more popular and accessible religion focused on *sants* and their centres, where large numbers of followers gathered whose initial religions or caste identity were not a barrier. Thus the equivalent of Dalits, who were denied entry to the sanctum of temples, could join the worship at Bhakti centres. In a few cases, they were refused this and it would be interesting to see the point at which this refusal was introduced. The subtle differences between the various teachings that we cluster together under the label of Bhakti need to be fine-tuned and their divergences explained.

At the base of Puranic Hinduism lay something of a paradox, also experienced by other religions undergoing similar processes. In order to spread and acquire a dominant status, the religion had to confront competition and perhaps ensuing conflict with other popular belief systems. Where the dominant religion wished to induct the lesser religious forms, it itself had to undergo some change. When the religion spread to new areas, as did Puranic Hinduism in the post-Gupta period, the existing elites could be converted to its beliefs and forms of worship and be allotted an attractive high status, but the lower castes received less attention and tended to continue their previous beliefs and practices. In some cases, there might have been a touch of Puranic Hinduism. The more immediate local forms continued and were occasionally even drawn into Puranic worship if thought to be significant by the authors. Diversity within the religion became essential and facilitated the process of a seeming amalgamation.

The control of the *brahmana* over this form of Hinduism differed from that over Vedic Brahmanism. Whereas the latter was pre-eminently the religion of the highest *varna*, and was kept secluded as such, Puranic Hinduism allowed the inclusion of diverse beliefs and forms of worship. The frequency of patronage became crucial as also did the participation of the worshipper. The priest remained dominant but in a different way.

Patronage for Vedic Brahmanism came from royalty and wealthy patrons, which meant that the *brahmana mathas* had an important function. Being recipients of largesse in the form of wealthy grants, they soon generated their own wealth as well. Royal and elite patronage to the *brahmana*, influencing aspects of Puranic Hinduism, was more through temples and their rituals but was no less generous.

Patronage to both the *mathas* and the *viharas* had meant that the learned elite could express themselves through writing and reading texts and that debate and discourse was the order of the day in these exclusive centres. Increasingly, Sanskrit became the language of discourse for both the Self and the Other, gradually reaching its greatest extent at a moment that was almost the prelude to the presence of the regional languages, initially almost imperceptible. This change ran parallel with the arrival of many facets of local cultures into the socially more elevated institutions. Dissent was perceptible now on at least two levels—in the intellectual discourses of the time and in the changes pertaining to religious forms.

Occasionally an older text such as a *Purana* dedicated to a particular deity would be adapted and recited but gradually new texts were composed in the newly emerging regional languages. Modern commentators have spoken of the *Bhagavad-Gita* as the essence of Hinduism, but although some of the Bhakti *sants* drew on it, the larger number had other sources for their teachings. Their message was not necessarily identical with that of the *Gita*. Some used other current teachings of the time.

The coming of Islam brought in further strands. Sunni Islam was associated with the courts of the Sultans but the Shias were not precluded even though there were conflicts between the two. Sufi teachers, largely from Central Asia, came as migrants who established their centres and a diversity of sects spread across the subcontinent. These were sects that often dissented from orthodox Islam and drew a large popular following. Their *dargahs* in particular became centres of worship and pilgrimage for a great number of people from non-Islamic religious backgrounds as well. However, in a few cases, the Sufi *pirs* were close to the centres of political power and received royal patronage.

Groups linked to some degree with Islamic belief and practice and emerging from yet more diverse origins were the many sects, of which some were descendants of Arab traders settled in the coastal areas with occupations tied to commerce, that kept them permanently in those areas. These were the Bohras, Khojas, Navayaths, Mapillas that I have mentioned earlier. A similar process was however taking place in some inland areas with the emergence of communities such as the Meos in Rajasthan and Haryana observing Islamic and Hindu festivals and rituals across the spectrum. It is problematic to generalize about religious identities at a subcontinental level prior to colonial times, since the identity of caste and sect reflected more often the particular religious observances of the region.

The coming of colonialism led to a dramatic change in these formulations of religion and a new imprint was imposed in categorizing the religions practised in India. Each was now seen as an overarching structure within which beliefs, codes and worship were force-fitted with attempts to emphasize uniformity. Hinduism was reconfigured by colonial scholarship and came to include everything non-Islamic barring Christianity and Zoroastrianism. The earlier history of dissent was incorporated into it as yet another aspect of an all-inclusive religion, or else it was ignored. The religions of the lower castes continued apace, but their study was treated as ethnography and the formulation of Hinduism was based largely on texts of the upper castes and their belief and practice. This latter had to be redefined and given a fresh shape in the context of changed politics.

Religion was not the only subject to be redefined. The European interest in this has been described as the search for an Oriental Renaissance motivated by the wish to find answers to current European problems from the experience and thought of the Orient. Indology was in part an answer to this and in part the effort to understand India. We also have to observe how far such studies were reflected in European thinking at that time, especially the European construction of what came to be called the Orient.

One of the weaknesses was that the Indological construction of Indian culture—the pattern of living—drew on the life and thought of upper-caste Indians but sieved through a colonial perspective. There were searches from the Indian for the values applauded in European civilization but somehow there was always a return to the specifically Indian that didn't quite match up. In time, the upper-caste Indians came round to treating the colonial perspective with some empathy. This could have been one of the reasons why little effort was made to see the relationship between the *varna* and *avarna* categories, across all the religions in India, nor was much attention given to the presence of dissent in the various cultures.

The colonial reading of Hinduism was suffused with the reading and study of Brahmanical texts, without seeing the limitations of this being the religion of a small although significant segment of society. The religion of this segment was not the religion practised by the whole of what was called Hindu society. What was not highlighted by the sources they consulted, and therefore not understood, was that the Hindu identified more immediately with sect and caste rather than an overarching religion. This gave flexibility to the identity. The intimate connection in India between caste and religion, irrespective of the particular religion, tended to be overlooked in the reconstruction of the religions. The institution that emerged encapsulating diverse forms of belief and worship was the sect that also provided a religious identity. The sects ranged across the span, some agreeing with and furthering existing religion and some dissenting from it.

Giving Hinduism institutions and organizations of a modern kind and different from the earlier ones began with establishing movements of socio-religious reform —the Brahmo Samaj, Prarthana Samaj, Sanatan Dharma and Arya Samaj—that led the regional middle classes to coalesce and give shape to what was assumed to be the best way of adapting the religion to contemporary requirements. This was a new kind of Hinduism that could be called Samajist Hinduism. It was an attempt to reconfigure the religion appealing largely to the upper- and middle-caste middle class. In a sense, it was a response to the colonial perspective of the religion. The *samajs* differed in their content and priorities. They were attempts at providing a new kind of institution that utilized the past to give direction to the current formulation of a religion more concerned with accommodating the needs of the current society. These *samajs* as institutions were also useful as feeders to support varieties of nationalism now beginning to enter the political discourse. Nationalism was being introduced to the various religious communities conforming to the map of Indian society as drawn up by colonial scholarship.

The *samajs* had their own limitations. They set out to reform upper-caste Hindu belief and practice in preparation for the social change implicit in the process of modernization. But it was difficult to entirely discard treating other prevalent religions as sources of impurity.

For instance, the Arya Samaj allowed Hindus converted to other religions to convert back, but they had to undergo the ritual of *shuddhi* / purification (rather like what today is called *ghar-wapasi*), the implications of which were obviously unacceptable to other religions. Nor does this illustrate the much-acclaimed sense of tolerance that modern Hindus boast of. The notion of purity-pollution was treated by upper castes as fundamental to Indian civilization. The religions most affected by the stigma of impurity were Islam and Christianity but there was little conversion back from these religions.

Despite the similarities in the *samajs*, there were differences; and since teachings were not identical, there were confrontations. The Sanatan Dharma and the Arya Samaj did not see eye to eye. The Sanatan Dharma or Eternal Dharma defined *dharma* as duties rather than religion; therefore, observing the *dharma-shastra* code was a requirement, as was relying on Brahmanical texts, especially the *Vedas*, postulating a single deity, believing in the existence of the soul and, therefore, in *karma* and rebirth, and permitting the worship of idols with rituals performed by *brahmanas*.

The Arya Samaj argued in favour of the superiority of the *Vedas* over all other texts, thus in a sense endorsing Vedic Brahmanism over Puranic Hinduism. In keeping with Vedic ritual, the worship of idols was not permitted. They had their own style of temple and priests in which icons were absent. Vegetarianism could be debated but beef was prohibited. Christianity and Islam were viewed as contrary to Hinduism. These *samajs* had a stronger missionary strand and were therefore active in socializing the new generation by setting up schools and colleges and emphasizing the recruiting of potential followers.

Because of political ambitions, the *samajs* had run-ins with other religious organizations with similar aspirations. Their concern with reforming some aspects of the Hindu religion initially had an impact on sections of the upper castes. These were ways of reviving support for the established religion but in new formulations. Curiously, the interest lay in addressing the upper castes. Less attention was given to the lower castes, nor was there much concern with the broader question of the interface of various religions in Indian society. The link to political aspirations was strengthened in the twentieth century with the knotting together of religion and nationalism.

As we have seen, if religion is used as a political agency, it must have some institutional base. This in turn can be the nucleus of an ideology for constructing a nation, but the religion has then to be reorganized in a way that meets this purpose. This emerged with the formulation of Hindutva that was and is the most recent attempt to reformulate the Hindu religion—this time as a monolithic, uniform religion with an unambiguous political purpose. The attempt at redefining Hinduism brought it into conformity with the colonial definition without ignoring political requirements of the last century; therefore all the sects—orthodox, heterodox, conservative, dissenting, opposed—were set aside so as to construct a particular Hinduism. The distinctions made by *brahmana* authors in medieval times of excluding the *nastikas* were no longer observed. The attempt was to reorganize it by introducing characteristics similar to the Abrahamic religions—Islam and Christianity.

The Hindu was identified by the fact of his ancestry and the origin of his religion coming from within the territories of India—the current British India—and the Hindu, being of the majority religion, was therefore the primary citizen. Hindus were said to be *aryas* and therefore the origin of the *aryas* also had to be within the territory of India for them to be indigenous to it. The problematic statement of Tilak, who spoke of the Aryans migrating to India from the Arctic, was got round by stating that in those days the North Pole was located in Bihar and therefore the Aryans were indigenous! (See the works of Bal Gangadhar Tilak and M. S. Golwalkar in Readings, Section 5.)

It is interesting that the question of territory became so fundamental to Hindutva since never before have there been territorial boundaries defining a Hindu or Hinduism as a religion. Territory is important to the concept of nationalism but not to religion. Defining territory is important to strengthening nationalism, so introducing it here makes it evident that Hindutva was and is intended to play the role of a political agency in nationalism. The link between nationalism and territory was common to many nationalisms but without the intervention of religion or language. Territorial precision was facilitated by cartography since boundaries can be drawn and redrawn on maps.

Hindutva is the ideological source of many linked groups that carry out political programmes such as the Rashtriya Swayamsevak Sangh, the Vishva Hindu Parishad, the Bajrang Dal, etc., the totality being referred to as the Sangh Parivar. The ideological content is limited since the emphasis is on a physical presence and on control. An innovation of recent times is congregational worship. Matters of belief and worship now come under the control of ecclesiastical authorities such as the *dharmasansads* of the *dharmacharyas*. It is a strongly missionary movement imitating the Christian missions with a massive number of *shakhas*, literally branches, spread across the country. It has also learnt from the Jesuits that education is a major channel of socialization, hence its many thousand schools. It also reaches out to Indians who have migrated to various parts of the world and who can be touched for impressive donations. The enviable flexibility of the earlier religion in its various phases has been leached out. Hindutva is not Hinduism as it was nor the religion as is.

Adherents tend to treat it as the most recent reformulation of Hinduism. It has parallels to the Abrahamic religions and is intended to facilitate the teleology of the Hindu Rashtra. Ancient teachers and founders are historicized, the beliefs are clear-cut, specific deities are chosen from the pantheon, and there is an attempt at a defining creed, at accepting a single sacred text and a belief in a uniform theory of rebirth. The Hindu was redefined as he who was born within the boundary of India as also was his religion. This gives him priority in the Hindu Rashtra. This redefinition by its very nature drew essentially from the upper-caste understanding of the religion, but in order for it to be used politically it needed to reach out to a bigger audience and be more attuned to the politics of the time. It is conveniently suitable to Hindu religious nationalism and the creation of the Hindu Rashtra. I have elsewhere called it Syndicated Hinduism, given the purpose for which it was invented. By this I am referring to its political agenda being strengthened by the emphasis given to Hindu nationalism, that is, nationalism dedicated to introduce a system in which the Hindus have priority. The political party and organizations required to do this inevitably follow.

There has been, in recent times, a debate on whether Hinduism can be described as having been invented in the nineteenth century because of the manner in which it was put together in colonial and associated thinking. I believe some are taking it further and arguing for the twentieth century. I would like to argue a different position. It was not a religion founded by a historical person and rooted, relatively unchanged, in historical continuity. It might be better categorized as a kind of agglutinative religion. Some forms were accretions, some led to the almost-unnoticed discarding of prior forms or at least their being marginalized. This was not unconnected to the religious articulations of various castes and communities. Its constituent parts therefore underwent mutation, modification and reformulation. These processes occur in the history of all religions. The amoeba-like accretions or breakaways had their own historical contexts and these are significant to its many phases that often surfaced in the form of sects. I have also argued that dissenting ideas as and when they arose were often responsible for mutations and reformulations perhaps to a larger degree than in many other religions. Hence the obvious plurality.

Some dissenting ideas were casual, others were more organized and took clear-cut forms. The instituting of Shramana sects as indeed also certain Bhakti sects as forms of dissent were decisive in their dissent and probably contributed more to the reformulations in established religions in India than we are prepared to admit. Given the diversity of sects and their increase in numbers over time, there was inevitably a multiplicity of dissenting groups. The articulation of dissent is crucial to the creativity of any religion, since debate takes ideas forward.

Sect and caste can be seen as more immediately relevant to religious identities than were the monolithic identities that we associate with religions, and this was so until almost recent centuries. Thus, Vedic Brahmanism has some continuity, although it has undergone alterations and is restricted to one *varna*—a small segment of society. Puranic Hinduism has had continuity but has also undergone some changes in belief and worship. Samajist Hinduism had its own context of caste and status, and each *samaj* remained largely regional in its initial ambitions. The ranks of the *avarnas* that constituted a sizeable population hosted the randomized worship of local deities and other forms of religious devotion, sometimes initially regarded as deviant. Religious articulation was substantially through the identity of the sect. It is the history, evolution and interface of the many sects that we should be investigating in the study of religion in India.

How was all this to be brought together? Was it actually brought together other than in theory? Hinduism was not invented in colonial times but an attempt was made to shuffle its reformulations and its many add-ons into a seemingly historical order and form. Voices of the Self and voices of the Other were bracketed into one even though the texts of the past had kept them separate. This ensured that the presence of the Other was discarded. In this process, it lost much that had made it a religion different from the Christianity of Europe and the Islam of West Asia, in that it had had pluralism and flexibility.

*

6. A Modern Movement of Dissent in the Context of the Nationalism of the Present

I shall now discuss a major moment of dissent that helped to establish a free and democratic India. I have chosen this because it draws on some of the earlier strands of the Self and the Other in the creation of dissent discussed in previous pages. It also questions the essentials of Syndicated Hinduism or Hindutva. We are all familiar with this form of dissent. It has been present in the cusp of our own times and has been much discussed over the past century. It is in some ways a partial coming together of elements of the earlier forms of dissent recognizable from the Indian past. These touch on the previous examples that I have presented. Nevertheless, it created its own contemporary form from these elements. Unlike my other examples, this one was aware of its ancestry in the thought and activities of past times as were those who responded to it. To that extent, it is somewhat different. I am referring to what Gandhi called *satyagraha*.

Since *satyagraha* was so integral to Indian nationalism, let me say a few words about nationalism. In India, its initial and overwhelming form was anti-colonial nationalism, a common experience to most erstwhile colonies. This implied the assertion of the free citizen ready to challenge political orthodoxies of various kinds that were inhibiting the freedom of the citizen. The construction of this identity recognizes that it is new.

Nevertheless, it has links from the past from which there is an implied legitimacy. So history becomes crucial. The experience of colonialism is in itself the experience of a historical change that alters the understanding that the individual has of himself or herself in the society that forms the context.

Nationalism, we must remember, is part of the historical change of considerable magnitude that has, in the last three centuries, altered the way the world sees itself. Together with industrialization, it belongs to the period that introduced radical new technologies whose functioning in many social activities was facilitated by the emergence of capitalism. Both these encouraged the evolving of the new middle class that controlled the change and consequently looked afresh at the society it had thereby constructed. At the level of knowledge, there were innovations in sciences, philosophies, religions, literatures and in the patterns of living.

One of the ways in which this change was articulated was through ideas of nationalism. Feudatory kingdoms or colonies that had framed the previous systems of governance belonged to another history and would have to be replaced by independent nation-states. Governance of the *praja* / subjects by the rajas of old or by the British Raj had to give way to the governance of a new category, the citizen. This was encapsulated in the interface between citizen and state through a government that was neither authoritarian nor alien but was representative of the citizens. That governance means representing the vision of the citizens was a departure from its earlier definition.

Not only was it to be a relationship between the citizen and the state that marked a departure from the past but it was also to be a relationship based on the citizen having rights, which rights were to be protected by the state. This new relationship was a contract between the citizen and the state and was recorded in the Constitution. Nationalism therefore was the coming together of all citizens who claimed equal status and rights to establish an independent nation-state. Since every citizen was involved, the nation could not discriminate between citizens on grounds of religion, ethnicity, language or any such identities. Therefore, nationalism based on the identity of religion that discriminated in favour of one religion lacked legitimacy as nationalism.

We may well ask why religious nationalism had a presence, although less significant, a century ago. It was in essence the response to colonial rule by those Indians who saw it as facilitating the making of a nation-state. In ascertaining the roots of Partition in 1947 and subsequent events, we quite correctly blame communal politics for the creation of the two nations; but in the process, we forget the deep imprint of colonial ideas.

As was common to most colonies, the colonial reading of the colony's earlier history that contributed to formulating its identity happened from the perspective of the colonizer. Some of this history was accepted by Indian anti-colonial nationalism but some of it was contested. The contestation contributed in part to the emergence of a legitimate anti-colonial nationalism. However, the colonial interpretation of this history resulted in two less legitimate forms, those of religious nationalisms. These were less legitimate because nationalism endorses a single all-inclusive identity, whereas religious nationalism endorses a deliberately selected identity that is not all-inclusive and excludes all but the one.

One may well ask why colonial thinking was at the root of religious nationalism. The colonial comprehension of India was founded on the two-nation theory. James Mill argued in 1817 that Indian history was essentially that of two nations—the Hindu and the Muslim—and that the two had been permanently hostile to each other. Colonial scholarship based itself on this idea and its implications and applied it to its studies of Indian history and society. History was periodized into three periods, the Hindu, the Muslim and the British. This periodization, essentially unhistorical, was given up half a century ago when the colonial view of history was questioned and much was discarded.

However, this colonial theory was loyally followed by both religious nationalisms—Muslim and Hindu. The concept of the Islamic state and of the Hindu Rashtra, the latter based on the Hindutva version of history, are each rooted in the colonial understanding of Indian history. Each of the two excluded the other and each distanced itself from anti-colonial nationalism.

The colonial propagation of the Muslim and Hindu nations provided the impetus for religious nationalism. The sectarian differences among sects claiming Islamic affiliation was easier to recognize, given that there were historical markers that gave it a structure. Dissident views were systematically suppressed, as they are to this day, in the attacks on Shias in places that have Sunni majorities, and such like. Mahmud of Ghazni's raid on the Shia mosque in Multan at the same time as his raid on Hindu temples should not come as a surprise, given the sectarian conflicts within Islam.

To project a Hindu nation required more planning since the historical markers to make a framework for it were obscure. This was done by re-interpreting the past and providing it with the teleology that its end purpose was the creation of a Hindu Rashtra / Hindu nation-state. This needed remoulding the religion into what was called Hindutva in such a manner that it would make the political mobilization of Hindus feasible and would simultaneously exclude the large number of minority communities. Parallel trends were emerging in the Muslim community that was the largest of the minority communities.

The reconfiguration encouraged a duality in nationalism: those that thought of nationalism as a secular, inclusive philosophy nurturing anti-colonial nationalism, as against those that thought of it as religious nationalism with its exclusive Hindu and Islamic components, each the counterpart of the other.

The broad-based anti-colonial nationalism obviously had a different agenda. It saw India as a nation of citizens who, irrespective of origins and with a substantially similar identity, were all of equal status and were coming together in the demand for an independent, secular, democratic nation-state. This was different from envisaging a primary or exclusive citizenship, as in the case of the two religious nationalisms. Nationalism, if defined by a single identity from among more, ceases to be nationalism and takes the form of majoritarianism, a form that is opposed to secular democracy and brings with it the threat of fascism. This seeks success by identifying a scapegoat, preferably a minority community, differentiated by religion or language, and which can be projected as the enemy within. In the last few years, attempts have been made by some to make the minority communities into scapegoats, attempts that have had some degree of success. Scapegoats are also required as a diversion when there is a failure in governance. We should keep in mind, however, that civilized societies do not treat any community as a scapegoat.

*

7. *Gandhi's* Satyagraha

Unlike the religious nationalisms, anti-colonial nationalism did not exclude dissent, neither in its own evolution nor in opposing colonial authority. This was one of the characteristics that differentiated anti-colonial nationalism from religious nationalisms. Anti-colonial nationalism accommodated various forms of opposition to colonial rule provided they did not give preference to a single identity. Among the more striking forms of Indian nationalism was the *satyagraha* of Gandhi. I say this because it seems to me that it echoes in some ways the earlier concepts of dissent that surfaced at various times in Indian history. But my interest in the form is concerned less with Gandhi's familiarity—or not—with these ideas in constructing *satyagraha*, and more with how they have always been a subconscious presence among the people of India. This is a subject that we need to focus on more than we have. My focus, therefore, is only partly on the thinking that was ancestral to the ideas that went into the meaning of *satyagraha* as given by Gandhi, some of which I have been discussing in this essay. My focus is far more on the question of what explains the overwhelming public response to Gandhi's *satyagraha*. How was it perceived by the people of India and why was there such an impressive response?

Perhaps the most widespread articulation of public dissent in India have been the Non-Cooperation and Civil Disobedience movements that were led by the Indian National Congress under the leadership of

Gandhi. They were what substantially became the push that came to shove in the Indian independence movement. Gandhi had read widely on Civil Disobedience, and from this as well as from his thinking on it there emerged what he called *satyagraha*—literally, the grasping of the truth, often translated as 'soul-force'. It was the right of refusal on the part of citizens to obey the commands and laws propagated by a particular government where the citizens regarded these commands as unlawful. The purpose here was for citizens to disallow the imposition of some of the laws of the British Indian colonial government. The purpose of Civil Disobedience was to counter these laws and explain why such action was being taken. The protest drew on moral justification as well.

In democratic societies this is a legitimate form of protest, but in dictatorships it is treated as illegal. The protest is not against all laws but only against particular laws. It is fundamental to the rights of the citizen and pointedly to the right to freedom of speech. The high point of Gandhi's call for Civil Disobedience was the Salt Satyagraha—getting salt from the sea, free of British intervention and taxes. This became the nucleus of a widespread protest.

Thinking about these movements as variations on the notion of dissent, the obvious questions are: Why was there such a powerful response and impressive endorsement of the implied dissent? Was it the symbolism of not using British-made goods or of producing the salt one needs? Were these the symbols that stirred the

Indian consciousness? Was it Gandhi's charisma and the trust that people had in his judgement? Was it the anti-colonial anger gathering force? Or was it that Indian society has always allowed an undercurrent of dissent that can be brought to the forefront when actions thought to be unlawful are being promulgated? An answer to these questions would require some exploration of the presence of dissent in Indian thought and activity since earlier times. This, in a sense, is what I have been exploring in this essay.

I would like to introduce a small personal note at this point and mention how my interest was touched even if not aroused. There was one occasion a lifetime ago when I very briefly met Gandhi and exchanged half a sentence on a simple matter. In a curious way, it seemed to touch a latent inclination on my part to go beyond the obvious, to search for what I like to call the context of thought and action.

I was in school in Pune in the early 1940s. Gandhi, when not in jail in Pune, would hold prayer meetings that we as young budding nationalists made it a point to attend. One evening, I took my autograph album to the meeting and, with much trepidation, requested Gandhi to sign in it. (There were no mobile phones in those days or else I might have asked for a selfie!) He signed in the book and, when handing it back to me, asked me why I was wearing a *salvar-kameez* of mill-made cloth and not of *khadi*, adding that I should only wear *khadi*. I readily agreed and assured him that I would do so. But what did *khadi* mean, other than its being a handspun and handwoven cotton textile, which Gandhi had converted into a symbol of economic independence through a distancing from industrialization? Was the displaying of dissent in a nonviolent way an assertion of confidence? Was wearing *khadi* a form of *satyagraha*?

The question was somewhat troubling as I did not see the immediate connection. As a young teenager, I had heard talk about what the colonial economy was doing to the existing Indian economy. The equally important issue of Civil Disobedience and Non-Cooperation was also being talked of and was associated with much that Gandhi suggested. It was treated largely as if it had suddenly sprouted virtually out of nowhere. The occasional and superficial links that were made with 'Indian values' were not convincing. This question remained unanswered in my mind until later when, searching for the context, I began to comprehend the meaning of *satyagraha*—and not just the concept but how it became relevant to anti-colonial nationalism. Even more important for me was how and why it resonated with the many who participated in the national movement. Without this resonance it would have remained just a slogan.

The events of the 1940s, the Quit India movement and the 'mutiny' in the Royal Indian Navy had their own message. Independence was imminent and the future was enveloped in debate. In what way was a colony going to be transformed into a secular democracy? What was going to be our identity as Indians, as free citizens? We would have a new relationship with the state—a state of our making. The Constitution was, in a sense, the covenant between the citizen and the state, recording the rights and obligations of each. Hovering over all these questions were those concerning the methods that we had used to attain independence. It was widely held that what marked our national movement as distinctive was the concept of *satyagraha*.

Over the years, I have asked myself why this concept became such a bedrock specifically in Indian anti-colonial nationalism. Predictably, it failed to find any place in the two religious nationalisms—the Hindu and the Muslim. These religious nationalisms converted the two religions into political agencies—the Muslim League supporting an Islamic state and the Hindutva version of Hinduism becoming the base for a Hindu Rashtra as projected by the Rashtriya Swayamsevak Sangh. In the politics of these concepts, the chickens of the colonial interpretation of Indian history and culture have come home to roost.

To understand this context, I have gone back in time and have tried to briefly trace the flow of some ideas that are regarded as foundational to Indian civilization. These have had a noticeable presence in Indian society for three millennia. Let me repeat what I have already said but with a slightly changed focus. Since religion has been politicized, I would like to look at the way in which we in our times have given shape to our religions. What is the form of dissent that we adopted and how does it link with religion in current times?

In the last two centuries, Indian religions have been reconstructed largely along the lines suggested by colonial scholarship. This was seldom seriously challenged and therefore came to be accepted. The popular focus has been on belief, ritual and texts, with little space for analysing the reach of religion into society as an agent of social and political consolidation or change. What social forms did it create or endorse and how might these have differed from what was there before? What was the interplay of conformity and dissent? These have been discussed in historical writing but haven't come sufficiently into public discourse.

As I have suggested earlier, when a religious teaching acquires a following, it establishes institutions that are initially places of worship—*chaityas, viharas, mandirs, ashramas, masjids, gurdwaras*, churches. Subsequently they can become institutions that bind. Monuments should be seen not just as architectural features of interest to architects and historians. They exercise control over those that use them as places of worship, and as institutions of socialization bonding society to religious norms. At this point, ideological support or opposition becomes a matter of asserting domination.

Religions in India were generally not viewed as monolithic, and especially not so in their practice. Religion was articulated more often in the form of a range of juxtaposed sects of which most were marginally linked with existing ones and some were distant. In pre-modern times, the religion of a person was identified more often by sect or caste and less frequently by an overarching label of Hindu or Muslim. Such labels come late in history. New sects and deities were created as and when required. Even in the last century, we saw the birth of a new deity in Santoshi Ma and a new sect following the Sai Baba, among others.

However, colonial perceptions of Indian religions projected a different format. Religious sects that seemed similar were bonded together under a few distinctive labels. Using the colonial binary of Hindu and Muslim, all religions that were not Muslim—barring Christianity and Zoroastrianism—were labelled Hindu, even those that in pre-colonial texts were listed clearly and distinctly as *nastika* and opposed to Hindu belief. The geographical identity mutated into a religious identity. This was mis-understanding the nature of religions in the Indian sub-continent. Territory does not define a religion.

Within the label of Hindu as defined by colonial scholarship, then, some sects contradicted each other's teaching and practice. The implications of this were ignored and uniformity was insisted on. The nineteenth-century middle-class interest in religion was largely con-fined to its own social boundaries, virtually unconcerned with the religions of those sections of society that are offi-cially called the Scheduled Castes, Scheduled Tribes and Other Backward Castes—SCs, STs and OBCs. Interest in the religion of these *avarnas*, those outside caste, was casual and of little importance in the definition of Hinduism or Islam or any other formal religion.

Not recognizing the role of diverse sects, some with a deep and some with a tenuous attachment to religion, each religion together with the sects as assumed attachments was treated as monolithic and uniform. Nor was it recognized that although every religion had adherents, it had also given rise to dissidents who questioned aspects of its belief and practice. Serious contradictions have been resolved at times only by changes in the code and creed. Despite this, religious conflict was present, but generally between the sects, for example, between the Vaishnava Bairagis and the Shaiva Dashnamis. Even now, dissenting opinions can evolve into marginal sects that find a place in the spectrum of religious sects, sometimes conspicuous and at other times unnoticed.

Sects shape the nature of Indian religions. Religions tend to be a collective of sects, some of whom are proximate to the orthodoxy and some far removed. Belief can be flexible and accommodating or contradictory. Adherence to code and creed links religion to society in which caste cannot be ignored. For the larger number of people in the past, the sect was a legitimate religious identity. Hence the facility in mixing religious observances among a range of sects, in the days when participation in religious activities was more open. This form militates against a unified, monolithic, overarching religious structure. Caste and region had a presence in the making of religious practice. Orthodoxy tended to gravitate to the core with dissenting groups at the periphery. Some degree of dissent was therefore always present.

The Shramana *dharmas* gave substantial attention to social ethics. This was expressed in their commitment to *ahimsa* / non-violence, to compassion and to working towards the social good. Social ethics were not absent in Brahmanism but tended to become ambivalent wherever the *dharma-shastras* were influential.

The dissenting ideas of the Shramanas were expressed in part by their beliefs that did not coincide with Brahmanism and in part by those of their practices that were alternate to that of established society. As I have said earlier, Shramanas as renouncers should not be confused with ascetics. The intention of each is different. It is a moot point whether Gandhi can properly be called an ascetic. That he was influenced by the philosophy of the renouncers would perhaps seem more accurate, and that is what I would like to argue.

Dissent did not lead only to the founding of renunciatory orders. It extended to discussing religion as an agency of social norms. The dissent of the renouncers took diverse forms, some of which were continued by the Bhakti *sants*. The views of some *sants* such as Kabir, Dadu, Ravidas, Chokhamela underlined social ethics and questioned caste. This would be expected from those who were themselves from the oppressed castes. We tend to set this aspect aside in our single-minded focus on religion. Historically, therefore, there was a continuing multiplicity in religious beliefs with some sects clearly dissenting from established views.

The sects of the renouncers, and later those with Bhakti and Sufi affiliations, were open to all and they could and did question the *dharma-shastra* codes, although perhaps not always in a direct way. Their vision of an alternate society would not be expected to come out of a violent social revolution. It envisaged social change resulting from a process of osmosis. It was essentially a way of stating and legitimizing dissent by persuading people to its ways of thinking, with an emphasis on social ethics and freedom to choose whom to worship. This freedom also imbued renouncers, *sants* and *pirs*, with a degree of moral authority in the eyes of people at large, a fact that was to play a significant role in the *satyagraha* movement. However, monks, *sants* and *pirs* were not regarded as saints. Moral authority should not be confused with saintliness. The idea of the saintly enters the discourse in colonial times. Social equality and justice were demands that were not readily supported by established religions except occasionally in theory. The act of renunciation was the expression of dissent. Nevertheless, non-Hindu religions that tended to become more formal, such as Islam and Sikhism, ended up segregating the converts of low-caste origin, the *pasmanda* and *mazhabi*.

Foremost in the ethical code of most renunciatory sects was negating violence of any kind. The concept of *ahimsa* negating violence is variously discussed and continues to be discussed. The other question is whether nonviolence is tied to bodily needs that might discourage violence. What was consumed as food, therefore, was important to some, for whom the diet had to be vegetarian. Fasting was a form of bodily purification and control. But undertaking a fast even to death for personal reasons was not the same as a fast in support of social protest.

*

8. The Social Articulation of Protest

The articulation of protest took diverse forms in different cultures and societies. Unlike in China and Europe, where peasant revolts of a violent kind were known, in India there are hardly any references to such revolts in the ancient period. However, the threat of agitation occasionally does hover. Peasant protest in earlier times took the form of peasants migrating to a neighbouring kingdom. We are told that kings feared such migrations since they resulted in a loss of revenue. In later times, there are some references to peasants and artisans threatening revolt.

Protests involving an urban population took other forms. One of these was included in the repertoire of Gandhi. It was known by various names, one among which was *dharna*, and was familiar to Rajasthan and Gujarat. Its success lay in its being undertaken by a particular category of people—the *charan* and *bhat*. These were bards, regarded as repositories of knowledge that was crucial to legitimizing the power of the ruler. This is another instance of people investing authority not in an officially designated person but in someone viewed as respected and integral to society. Today, with a shift to excessive reliance on formal authority, this category of protest has become less effective with the bards not performing this earlier function or, at any rate, not in such an apparent manner. However, recognizing their role in earlier times provides a glimpse of how societies operated not so long ago.

Some activities of these bards were essential to power. Authority needs constant legitimation. The bards maintained the genealogies of the rulers and occasionally of the important functionaries, through which they became the keepers of the history of the dynasty. The status of those in authority was asserted by the *charan* through alluding to the believed historical evidence of clan and caste. The *charans* themselves had a low social status, but since early times they were respected as inviolate, and were also called upon to arbitrate in disputes.

Authority is of various kinds. In some situations, moral authority can take precedence over the political. It goes with the belief that a particular kind of person, being what he is and what he does, has moral authority. The *charan* had it. He would take up the protest of the people once he was convinced of its legitimacy. To support the protest, he would position himself at the threshold of the royal residence and go on a hunger strike / fast, until there was a resolution of the conflict or, alternatively, he was close to death by voluntary starvation.

The effectiveness of the fast was dependent on the fasting person being someone who commanded moral authority, who was respected by both rulers and subjects. His power was intangible but based on this respect. His protest was legitimate if it focused on a demand for justice. If the *charan* lost his life owing to the fast, the ruler was doomed. Thus the moral threat posed by the fast was feared. The dual purpose of the fast as dissent and as a moral threat was not unknown in earlier forms of registering protest. The fast subsumed the protest and diverted it from becoming violent.

Can one see in this some parallels to the use of the fast by Gandhi? The British Raj may not have admitted it publicly but each of his fasts was a matter of anxiety to their political control, since he was the leading national figure. The title of *mahatma* in turn recognized his moral authority with the people. The fast was a protest against injustice but also carried a grave threat should it have taken its toll. This was well understood. Gandhi's projection of nonviolent protest introduced it as a component of the national movement. The inability to always conform to nonviolence became a crucial issue.

*

9. *Did the Public Response to* Satyagraha *Come Out of an Embedded Tradition of Dissenting Forms?*

Let me turn to the implications of this activity. Dissent of various degrees was at the core of the tradition of renunciation as indeed also at the core of the teaching of some *sants*. Can we then ask whether the public endorsement of Gandhi's *satyagraha* drew to some degree from this tradition either consciously or subconsciously? Let me repeat that I am less concerned with the ancestry of the idea of *satyagraha* as constructed by Gandhi, and more with why it brought about a positive response from the Indian public. More central to my argument is the thought that an evident strand of dissent that had emerged from the concern for social ethics in the philosophy of renunciation, and some of the thinking of the *sants* searching for social justice, probably encouraged the public response to *satyagraha*. Does the essence of Shramana renunciation together with the later Bhakti and Sufi strand of individual self-definition link to some degree with the resonance of the Indian people to Gandhi's *satyagraha*?

The peasant movements in UP (what was then called the United Province) and Bihar in the first half of the twentieth century had among their more prominent participants and leaders people such as Baba Ramchander of Avadh and Sahajanand Saraswati, identified popularly as *samnyasi* and *sadhu*. Whatever their antecedents may have been—and they were diverse—they were not averse to a hint, sometimes more than a hint, of the renouncer as a figure evoking dissent. In this case, there was more than dissent since the protest was against taxes and demands from both the landlords and the administration. These movements have been narrated and debated at length by historians, to whose writings I refer.

For instance, 1921 saw massive rallies by peasants in the Gorakhpur area of UP. Gandhi's words and actions were the focus of frequent conversations. Reported and recorded by the administration, they have now been used to support an account of how Gandhi was viewed by the populace. It was said that he had taken a vow of renunciation—*samnyas-vrat*—for the well-being of all. He is referred to sometimes as Guru Gandhi in the best Bhakti tradition. Some activities attributed to him are those associated with *sadhus*. He is believed to have performed miracles—again something linked to 'holy men'. It is interesting that the miracle worker is not seen as a member of the *raiees*, the gentry, nor as a *brahmana* (even though some peasant leaders had such origins), but as a person who began as 'one of us' and came to be acknowledged as a *mahatma*. The *brahmana* performed rituals, not miracles. But the believed-in miraculous powers of Gandhi are similar to those often mentioned together with renouncers and ascetics. The fantasies on which miracles are based are of course common to all religions. On the more practical side, but believed with equal fervour, was the conviction that Gandhi would persuade the British government to reduce the rents and taxes that the peasants had to pay.

Gandhi's definition of the concept of *satyagraha* drew from the authors he read and wrote about and this has been much discussed: Tolstoy, Thoreau and Ruskin in particular. He had lengthy conversations with Raichandbhai on the Jaina religion, as he would also have done with his mother and others in Gujarat that was partial to Jainism. He read many texts of the Bhakti *sants* as well, especially those of the fifteenth-century Narsi Mehta in Gujarati. My attempt is to understand what it was that struck a public chord in this particular form of protest.

Gandhi's reading of texts closely associated with Hinduism was of a different genre, for example, his careful reading of the *Gita* and the attraction of *brahmacharya*. Could the prevalence of alternative cultural patterns from the past have nudged him into seeking a practice that would be seen as the outcome of thoughts that flourished as part of a perceived tradition? The imprint may have been less apparent than we have realized, both on him and his audience. Did the form of and justification for *satyagraha* reach out to a stronger tradition of expressing dissent? Some have argued that it was the ideal of *brahmacharya* that he was emulating. But *brahmacharya* was not born out of protest and dissent. It was a way of life acceptable to orthodoxy and, like asceticism, was the self-expression of the individual. It focused more on individual liberation from rebirth, rather than on social ethics. It denied women a place of significance. *Satyagraha* differed, as it was primarily a political statement. I am not suggesting that the Indian tradition was foremost in the making of Gandhi's thoughts and actions, but, rather, that there were prevailing cultural patterns that may have subconsciously facilitated the internalization of his ideas. More than that, it gave to the person responding to Gandhi a sense of recognizing the continuity of a pattern in making manifest particular thoughts and actions.

Parallels with renouncers are more noticeable in the making of the practitioner, the *satyagrahi*. To be effective, a period of training was preferred, although there were some exceptions of a few persons that were exempt. There is some mention of taking vows or consenting to observe certain rules. Once accepted, the discipline of living in the *ashrama* was reasonably strict. This is also borne out in the memoirs of one young woman, Manuben. *Satyagraha* was not a monastic order. Nevertheless, it had its own rules, relationships and identity. One can perhaps see a subconscious attempt at adjusting the teaching into a slight semblance of discipline, to possibly taking it in the direction of an institution. This would prevent Civil Disobedience from becoming a runaway activity.

To assert a greater moral force, it was preferable that the *satyagrahi* be celibate, although this was not insisted upon. Protest included the nonviolent *swadeshi* movement—observing the boycott of foreign goods, especially cloth that was not unconnected to industrialization in Britain. This was a part of Civil Disobedience that of course had much broader concerns. The wearing of *khadi* and objections to mill-made cloth was not intended as a Luddite movement but as registering another form of dissent and explaining why it was necessary.

Some symbols of renunciation also surface. Underlying *satyagraha* lay the force of moral authority—soul-force—of the person calling for civil disobedience and the response. This, in a sense, echoed what also gave authority to renouncers of various kinds, and in diverse ways. That Gandhi was named a *mahatma,* an honour that interestingly he did not reject, was partly a recognition of his moral authority. Such authority required neither an office nor an official status. Its strength lay in the teaching that endorsed social ethics as necessary to society. Its force lay with those that accepted the leadership of the person who asserted it.

A fundamental requirement of *satyagraha,* as also in the Shramana religions, was to refrain from using violence. The use of violence or even the observable dependence on violence destroys moral authority. *Ahimsa* faced the opposition of the colonial power and its continued violence against anti-colonial nationalist protesters. Those that shouted slogans such as 'Inquilab Zindabad' and 'Azadi' were *lathi*-charged, arrested and jailed under British rule. Violence and the exercise of power are interconnected at many levels and on many occasions. This brings violence into the realm of political activity. The use of violence when it is qualified, which can be called contingent or conditional violence—for instance in the *Gita*, where violence is permitted if it is destroying evil—frequently relates to the political sphere, from assassinations to battles. Kings, commanders and soldiers, even when they were Buddhists and Jainas, did not allow the vow of *ahimsa* to stop them from killing the enemy.

The commitment to nonviolence and truth underlined the idea of tolerance. The need for tolerance was a statement repeated by rulers over the centuries which suggests that neither could tolerance be taken for granted nor was it invariably prevalent. It is frequently missing among those greedy for power. Had tolerance prevailed, there would not have been a need to evoke it repeatedly. Not entirely unrelated to the concept of *ahimsa* was the other that Gandhi often emphasized, namely, *nishkama karma*. The latter has been discussed as the idea of action that does not take into account personal gain. If this can be extended to include the ethics of ends and of means and the individual's responsibility for his or her actions, then the link to *ahimsa* becomes more pertinent.

Most sects of renouncers were not concerned with overthrowing the existing system but with setting up an improved alternative, at least initially. They also had ideas about the kind of society they wanted and envisaged it by redefining the reality. They knew the present and had ideas about the future. They were people with a vision. The vision is often the cynosure of ideology. One is also reminded of the Bhakti *sant* Ravidas who envisioned a society where everyone was equal, and this for him would remove the central cause of sorrow.

All religions were to be equally respected. Presumably, this endorsed equal rights essential to *satyagraha*. The latter did not have its own singular religious identity, although one of the religions in its practice was perhaps more equal than others. However, there was a moral right to break the law if it caused widespread suffering. But who had the right to judge? Was Gandhi assuming this right strengthened by being called a *mahatma*? The dilemma becomes more acute if one accepts what one may call the contingent or the conditional *ahimsa* of the *Gita*, that violence is permitted if the fight is against prevailing evil. Yet the *satyagrahi* has to persuade the other to his view in nonviolent ways and through a system where the means and ends are not contradictory.

Violence does not persuade; it replaces persuasion by fear and terror. In the process, it sadly negates the quality of the human in those asserting authority and the fear of violence encourages those being subjugated to accept the negation. The negation often remains at the level of a substratum and is not spoken about. Yet it is crucial that it have a presence as an ethical necessity in all relationships involving the balancing of power. Its negation allows those with power to treat those being subjugated with contempt. Would Gandhi's generation and his immediate successors have referred to those subjugated as 'termites'?

A more complicated issue was present when *satyagraha* was practised in the larger social context. This involved the equality of all castes, including the outcastes. Did the equal status of all castes as maintained by some dissenting sects apply to both the *varna* and *avarna* members of society or only to the former? How was the hierarchy to be countered in practice? Gandhi was aware of the implications but a solution remained distant. It touched not only on one's present life, but if one believed in rebirth, as many did, then also on one's life to come. Many maintain that the actions of one's previous life determine one's birth in this life. But if actions are evaluated by caste and in accordance with the *dharma-shastra* codes, then the codes would have to be unhesitatingly discarded if the hierarchy of caste is to be annulled. But few argued for this.

The Shramana sects claimed that the monasteries did not observe the rules of caste. On a wider social scale, it was some of the Bhakti *sants* who also opposed caste, particularly those who came from the lowest castes. For Gandhi, if the *varna* castes began doing the demeaning jobs allotted to the *avarnas*, the stigma might go. But caste by now had many ramifications other than just this, and this was inadequate. Unlike the renouncer, the *satyagrahi* was not asked to annul his caste identity.

The appeal of *satyagraha* is evident from the large numbers that responded when the call was given for civil disobedience. We have to ask what went into the making of this form of defiance. Could there have been an echo of the persistence of dissent that still surfaced when injustice was experienced? It galvanized national sentiment, but it also diverted this sentiment away from violent revolution, when it came to channelling it into protest. This was true to type, as such movements even in the past had steered away from violent revolution. Is it possible to argue that because opposing explanations took recourse to becoming a sect placed in juxtaposition to other sects, there was more likelihood of sectarian conflicts rather than widespread violence between formal religions?

In the colonial situation, *satyagraha* gave the protesters and the reason for the protest—irrespective of whether they were protesting over salt or cloth or the freedom of a people—a marked visibility. This is what the protesters wanted but the authorities did not. Visibility is a source of strength in civil disobedience. This kind of dissent underlined a claim to status by the colonized by forefronting moral authority against colonial power. This was outside the experience of the colonizer.

Admittedly, Gandhi in his readings lists little that goes back to the texts of the Shramanas. His formal interest in such sources seems marginal, especially compared with his intensive study of the *Bhagavad-Gita*. However, that *satyagraha* could envelop dissent rather than violent protest suggests that these ideas had a presence, however inaudible. Given the complexities of thought, of society and of politics in India in the first half of the twentieth century, it would seem that a major player on the scene may have held on to the truth of some forms of dissent from the Indian past and used them almost instinctively to recreate a new form of dissent. The acceptance of this is impressive.

One could ask whether Gandhi's endorsement of the *Gita* contradicted the insistence on nonviolence in *satyagraha*. The translation he began with—apart from the Gujarati—was the English translation by Edwin Arnold, *The Song Celestial*, published in 1885 and much read at that time. The potential of the *Gita* to be the single sacred book of Hinduism, the equivalent of the Bible and the Quran, was part of contemporary discussions.

The *Gita*, together with the sections that were added to the original, has been analysed historically and are thought to date to around the turn of the Christian era. There were regular commentaries on the text throughout the centuries. It surfaced as more than ordinarily important in the nineteenth century and rode the European Orientalist wave that was searching for wisdom from the East. The Theosophists adopted it as a central text and gave it wide diffusion. Some saw it as an allegory and this excluded questions of historicity. W. B. Yeats, T. S. Eliot and Christopher Isherwood all flirted with its ideas.

It was appropriated by many nationalists such as Aurobindo and Tilak possibly because it could be used to endorse even violent political action as the duty of those fighting for rightful demands and justice. If colonial rule was evil, then violence against it was justified. Anti-colonial nationalism was itself a form of dissent against the colonial government. The message of the *Gita* focuses on the liberation of the individual and the dilemmas faced by a person confronting various problems. Solving problems at a social level is not its primary intention. It is not presenting a vision of an alternate society.

What is perhaps curious is that the *Gita* was drawn on so heavily for questions relating to violence and political action. As some have pointed out, a more appropriate text would have been the twelfth book of the Shanti Parvan of the *Mahabharata* that unambiguously focuses precisely on this theme. This segment of the epic is taken as a later insertion and dated generally to the post-Mauryan period. The text narrates that subsequent to the battle at Kurukshetra, Yudhishthira was expected to take up the kingship, but he initially refused to do so, preferring to retire to the forest. His objection to ruling was that kingship involves many levels of violence and killing, from the royal hunt to the endless campaigns, and he was averse to these.

Yudhishthira questioned the description of a war as *dharmic* when it is the duty of some such as the *kshatriya* to kill others. His grandfather Bhishma, still lying on a bed of arrows from the battle, justified such killing as the ruler needing to defend and protect the realm. This conversation is a fine example of dissent explored through debate. Yudhishthira eventually agreed to be the raja—although one suspects with a heavy heart.

Those for whom *ahimsa* was an absolute commitment with no conditions attached would naturally differ from those for whom *ahimsa* was contingent or conditional, as it was in the *Gita*. Yudhishthira has a moral and ethical objection to violence. This debate could reflect the discussions on violence at the time, enhanced perhaps as has been argued by various scholars by the views of Emperor Ashoka in support of *ahimsa* as a significant component of *dhamma*. (See, for example, the works by J. L. Fitzgerald and N. Sutton in Readings, Section 9.) Was the centrality of *ahimsa* in this conversation with the conditionality that circumscribes it somewhat, a concession to the then-current Shramanic debate? Unlike Nehru, Gandhi's interest in the Buddha and Buddhism was relatively limited. Nor was he particularly interested in a sequential study of the past. History was perhaps not a subject that provoked him intellectually as it did Nehru.

That there were occasions of violent and intolerant actions in our past is undeniable. That there were also legitimate traditions of nonviolent dissent is also undeniable. The forms of the latter changed in conformity with a changing society and we have to recognize the forms and how they were used and when. Gandhi created a variant form of dissent as others had done before him. Yudhishthira's statements on political violence seem to argue that when religious ideas and their implications become agencies of political mobilization, their fundamental purpose changes. The political determines thoughts and actions. The continuation of the right to dissent, to disagree, to debate can be seen in the varied manner in which it has been formulated. *Satyagraha* has been one effective form in recent times.

EPILOGUE | *Should We Remember Our Many Voices of Dissent from the Past and Hear Them Speak to Us Today?*

I have tried to show that dissent, disagreement, difference of opinion have all not only been present in the Indian past but have also, through their interaction with existing ideas and practices, contributed to creating new idioms that have been crucial to the making of what we today call Indian civilization, patterns of living, cultures, traditions—call them what you will. To recognize forms of dissent and observe their interaction with society is essential to understanding the outcome of conversations both of the past and of the present that hover around the Self and the Other, and speak of conservatism and dissent; to encourage us to look at how we envisage the present and what it portends of the future; to validate the political roots of our attempts to establish a secular democratic society and, above all, a just society.

I have tried to argue that in earlier times dissent was often, but not always, expressed through various forms of renunciation, or by establishing a new sect with an alternative message. In pre-modern times, this frequently involved a religious idiom as it was easily recognized and had a social outreach. We should learn to read not only its religious message but also what it wished to convey in a wider context.

Modern times have experienced the coming of nationalism that is part of an elemental change in society.

Inevitably, dissent today expresses new aspirations, although the avenues of dissent may remain familiar or may take new forms. The coming of the nation-state, the struggle for its autonomy and the replacing of slaves, serfs and subjects by the free citizen with full rights introduces a new vision of the present and the future. Dissent no longer needs to use the idiom of religion and can now use the idiom of civil society, and the subject at issue is that of the rights of citizens. This historical mutation has to be understood, recognized and appreciated both by those governing and those being governed. Dissent can still use some of the older avenues as was clear from their quick recognition in the last century. But it must also introduce the new avenues necessary in the changed context.

We have to learn to expect and accept dissenting views and discuss them—not silence them. Dissent in our time must be audible, distinct, opposed to injustice and supportive of democratic rights. The articulation of dissent does not mean a violent revolution. It is a civilized discourse on disturbing questions that need answers.

Forms of dissent are not imports into Indian thinking from the West as has been and is argued by those unwilling to explore the implications of dissent in a society. Nor does dissent ride in only on the backs of rational philosophies. Its origins lie in a multiplicity of ideas that come from diverse ways of thought and from manifold lived experiences. These ideas range from the many debates in the Indian philosophical tradition to the teachings of those who mingled with the populace and preached what they envisaged as living worthwhile lives.

I have taken three historical examples to illustrate my thoughts, each separated by a millennium, and each initially projected as a category of the Other. As such, they implicitly formed epicentres of dissent. From the simple duality of the first example, there was a contrast in the second and the third with layers of Otherness and their multiple manifestations addressing a range of those articulating the views of the Selves. The changing historical context also requires us to consider the difference from earlier times. Some ideas were opposed and rejected, some were subsumed into the thinking of the dominant society and some were accommodated as yet another juxtaposed sect, whether willingly or not. We need to know what social relationships emerged from these procedures. How were they viewed? Equally important is the question that we rarely ask: How did the various sects on their part view these social relationships? What would be the view of these historical moments from the perspective of the Others?

We tend to view our past cultures largely through the lens of the established Self at differing times in history. It is comfortable and convenient to do so. Or else we inflict our present-day stereotypes on the past without examining their viability, for instance, when we inflict binary identities on the past where they did not exist in the way we envisage them. We give weightage to the texts of those in authority, be it royalty or sections of the elite or scholars of religion, marginalizing the views of others. Who, after all, are the majority practitioners of a religion? In defining our traditions and our cultural inheritance, where the view of the Other should have a significant presence, we allow it to recede both in what was accommodated and in what was contested, and give little reason as to why we do so. Yet this would be a necessary perspective.

Understanding the interface between religion and society requires us to recognize that both the formal religions and the more informal evolving sects were being continually transformed in the process of addressing society. In the process, neither remained unchanged and change was and is in itself a continuous process. New thinking arises either to further confirm what is, or to contest it in varying degrees. The Self cannot be understood without the Other, and the Other cannot be set aside. Where identities are strongly demarcated, there the presence of the Other tends to be more visible, defining identities and social gradations. This is as true of the past as it is of today.

Religion is only one marker of identity. It has to be conjugated with other markers—occupation, caste and social status, language, region, the environmental context, and so on. Each religion therefore has to be related to its larger social constituency together with whatever changes it undergoes. Why do some religious sects that initially take form as the Other become part of the Self? The Lingayats became a powerful presence in society whereas, by comparison, the Kabirpanthis lost out. The answer is not limited to observations on what they taught but also how they related to various social communities and vice versa.

Religions are never static. Societies change, so do the religions linked to these societies, because religious identities never arise in isolation. Some are viewed as heritage and some as a reaction to the Other, be it from within society or from outside. A formal religion becomes difficult to define if it has a multiplicity of sects sensitive to and reacting to change, and sometimes overlapping at the edge of each. They often begin in the form of the Other asking questions or presenting alternatives. If the Shaiva Dashnamis and the Vaishnava Bairagis were in disagreement relating to the Puranic religion, so were the Barelvis and the Deobandis in relation to the Quranic religion. What continues, what changes, and why—that is what we are searching for, and the search is perennial.

Religious expression varies from one segment of society to another. Those at the lower end were and are the largest in number and sustain a substantial culture. But in these groups religion is even more diverse in belief and practice and this in turn gives it greater flexibility. Social and religious identities were and are more strongly demarcated among the elite that have always been the minority in terms of numbers. There is generally more overlapping in the sects of the larger numbers, despite some exceptions. But identities are not formed entirely in isolation. They are constantly mutating irrespective of their origins. This process is a kind of cultural symbiosis particularly where the interface is between initially distinctive cultures.

We assume the dominance of one religion and treat it as drawing in a range of others or else we isolate the one that we like to think of today as altogether separate. We treat medieval history as the period of the dominance of Islam in India, ignoring the way in which religions of every kind were shaped at this time given their intensive interactions. The many takes of Bhakti began in South India in the later first millennium AD, but they became an even more significant subcontinental face in the second millennium and in some areas ruled by the Turushkas. Some initially Islamic institutions took different forms when faced with a range of Selves and Others. Why was this change necessary?

I have tried to suggest that our treatment of this period as a rigid formalized binary makes it incapable of explaining the interface of a range of Selves with a range of Others that were characteristic of our history. Binaries make for obfuscation and wipe out the necessary nuances. It was from among the multiple sects surfacing across the spectrum and in the process of negotiating their space that there arose accommodations, or contestations or a juxtaposed coexistence. The nature of dissent therefore altered as it moved across the spectrum. The three examples I gave were of initially conflicting situations resolved ultimately into accommodation or juxtaposition through creating new forms.

These in turn made way for other forms of dissent or accommodation.

It is not enough to point out that there has always been an Other or Others, as there have been many Selves in Indian thought and practice. The reasons for each have to be analysed in the light of mutating identities. Where the Other is a voice of dissent, there the acknowledgement of this dissent is essential because, by its very nature, it also reflects the perception that we have of ourselves, irrespective of the culture with which we claim identity. Many sects either juxtaposed to or even distant from one another represent complex and divergent thoughts that have in the past sculpted the Self and the Other. This allowed a free play of belief, emotion and enquiry, such that they invalidate our present-day obsession with singular, monolithic, binary identities. It is to this tradition of the dissent of the Other and its interplay with the Self that we owe many moments of spectacular thinking that are evident in the dialogues of agreement or of dissent in multiple literary and philosophical genres.

Speaking of the continuities of dissent, let me bring the narrative up to present times and mention what I believe has been a deep echo and a contemporary version of the kind of dissent that we have frequently experienced in times not so long ago. In many ways, it takes forward the Gandhian *satyagraha* but in a different context. I am referring to the demonstration against the Citizenship Amendment Act / CAA and the National Register of Citizens / NRC that began at Shaheen Bagh in New

Delhi and then sprang up across the country in the form of multiple local versions of Shaheen Bagh. It was only the spread of Covid-19 that brought it to a closure.

I visited Shaheen Bagh one morning with a couple of friends and sat and chatted with some of the women who were sitting in protest. It was largely a gathering of women, many of them Muslim. From my conversations with them, it was clear that they knew precisely what they were protesting about and what the implications were of the CAA. Their plea was that their fears should be discussed with them and that they should be given an assurance that their citizenship rights would not be annulled. They were not protesting against the state and they were not supporting terrorists. It was a justified request considering the sorrow caused by the confusion in Assam over this and related issues.

I left Shaheen Bagh deeply moved both by the dignity of the women who were protesting and their intensely felt concerns. Although extensive in numbers, it was a quiet, almost disciplined protest with a very occasional speech requesting dialogue on their anxieties, and a singing of the national anthem. The speeches were few and the quiet conversations were many and were noticeably civilized. There was no vulgar abusive language, no calls for killing people as was heard from some senior politicians elsewhere. The Shaheen Bagh protest was strictly nonviolent. It was particularly impressive as the articulation of women from all backgrounds, and more so from backgrounds where they have been stifled in this country and many continue to be. As an Indian woman, I felt proud of the women who were my compatriots and were speaking with such conviction on the legitimacy of their protest.

This movement and the many others like it that it generated took form at a point in historical time that marks a change in urban middle-class Indian society, organized and participated in by women. That women should speak up on an issue tied to birth and citizenship makes perfectly good sense. It is almost predictable. Even if it is taken symbolically, we know that only the mother can speak with authority about the identity of the child and its place of birth.

Equally significant was the fact that it was a movement that did not use the idiom of religion. Theirs was a secular articulation of a kind that one associates with the rights that should come with citizenship. I felt after many years that I was witnessing a form of dissent that was somehow taking off from the roots of anti-colonial nationalism. There was no mistaking its all-inclusive character. It took me back to the 1940s and to my very youthful participation in anti-colonial nationalism!

As women, they were holding their own and with great courage. Individuals and groups of people of the minority communities—more particularly Muslims and Christians—are easily targeted these days. They belong to religions that originated in places outside the boundaries of India, and are therefore alien according to Hindutva. The Dalits are also targeted for being uppity in demanding just a fraction of their rights as citizens. This is illustrated in the history of many countries in the last century. In conditions of unrest, they can be made into the scapegoat communities accused of creating the unrest.

It is on occasions such as this that one can see with clarity the difference between democratic governance and governance disinterested in what makes citizens anxious about their existence. Should there not be dialogue between those governing and those being governed? We should revive the system that once existed in democracies when there could on occasion be dialogue between government and citizens, and this not just through the legislative bodies but also through conversations between citizens and elected legislators. There is no shortage of subjects and policies that need discussion. There are enough members of the executive—the many branches of the administration and those controlling law and order—that should be in dialogue with the society which they are meant to be serving. The judiciary is so fashioned as to be an independent institution that checks any excesses of the others in governance. When these three institutions that uphold democracy fail to function as intended by the Constitution, then citizenship suffers and democracy fades away.

Civil disobedience is not inimical to democracy. In fact, it has an additional use in reminding these three institutions of the functioning expected of them. What filled me with hope was the feeling that the particular expression of dissent that I have always associated with all that was best in our society still resonates with our people. Civil disobedience as one form of dissent was not just an anti-colonial activity or an act of disobedience. Its potential as dissent was known in pre-colonial times and it persists and can still speak to us, both the governed and those governing, provided it is not silenced. What also filled me with hope for the future was the extensive support for this movement from the young. For them, too, it was a legitimate expression of dissent. Students and other young people came from a variety of backgrounds to join in. It is always the future of the young that is at stake since the future inevitably lies with the young and they have to know how to protect it. The shape of things being what they are the need for protection is apparent.

The expression of dissent is usually projected as a law-and-order problem. This it cannot be if it is not a violent protest disrupting the functioning of every life. It does not require to be met with state terror. What it requires is dialogue between the dissenters and those with whom they are in disagreement. Dissent has to be the subject of a dialogue and not the reason for encouraging brutality. The enforcement of law and order becomes entirely ineffective if people are terrorized. This has often been demonstrated and most recently again in the riots that swept across the cities of the USA under the banner of Black Lives Matter.

The kind of dissent I have discussed has prevailed and continues to be present. It has succeeded or failed because of the particular configuration of the society it addressed as I have tried to argue. It is not intended to overthrow states and governments. Those that support it are not terrorists. It does insist that where necessary societies must change for the better and it points to that which prevents such change. Above all else and most importantly, it insists on reminding us that human societies cannot survive without a code of ethics, a code that is agreed to both by those governing and those being governed. Such a code should not remain a code in theory but must be practised to ensure the nurturing and the protecting of all citizens that constitute the society. We know from history that systems with a limited agenda of protecting only those that have wealth or that conform to a particular belief system or any other single identity will inevitably fail as they have done consistently in the past.

The ethical code demands an open dialogue between those governed and those governing, between citizens and those in institutions of authority. Governments are appointed to nurture and protect the rights of all the citizens, not just of a select few. The function of dissent has to be understood as what was inherently a moral force that gave people the strength to assert their humanity.

In many ways, the right to dissent has been highlighted by the coming of the nation-state. Free speech and the right to dissent is an essential requirement in the definition of the free citizen as is her right to call for discussion and explanation. It registers the substantial change in the historical context, the new historical phase involving the rights of the citizen and the obligations of the state. The citizen is no longer the *praja* / the child, to those that govern. The contractual relationship between the state and the citizen, embodied in the Constitution, gives the citizen specific rights that the state must honour. Honouring rights and duties is an ethical obligation on the part of each. If the citizen is to honour his or her duties to the state by not being anti-state, then the state must also honour the rights of the citizen by not encouraging the citizen to fear the state. The mutual commitments of state and citizen cannot be ignored.

Dissent has been expressed in many forms and this range will continue and, in fact, be added to. The expression has moved in the past from the idiom of a religious form to one that relates to civil rights. New idioms will be required as, for instance, with the recent debates on the destruction of the environment and its links to climate change. These are all issues of immediate importance, but some call for more detailed discussions. The rights of citizens are of course the most immediate and the priorities in these rights will doubtless be subjected to contestation. This is where a vision and its defence will be crucial. If we are to survive into a future that is worth waiting for, then the provision and maintenance of basic human rights will be the first requirement.

It remains open to the citizen immersed in the ideology of secular democracy to articulate this new relationship by reiterating these rights. And it needs those that speak for the state—those in authority in all the civic institutions—to acknowledge the validity of this right. Among the trajectories from the past as recorded in history is the one pointing to the voice of the citizen gradually becoming more audible. When citizens have spoken up, as in recent history, and expressed dissent, the state has often been unable to silence them and has had to hear what they have to say. The future can only lie in the state and citizen being in effective dialogue to ensure the rights and duties each have to the other.

INTERVIEWS

1. *With Rohan Venkataramakrishnan for* Scroll.in

You note at various points in the book that dissent has a very Indian history, situated here, rather than as something brought to India from afar. Is that what drove you to write this book?

Dissent is not exclusively Indian but is present in India as it is elsewhere, in every society and civilization, and relates to ideas, theories, practices and beliefs. There is, of course, a more obvious consciousness of it in the exploration of knowledge and philosophical discussion. The latter in the Indian past almost began with inquiries about the views and opinions of 'the Other' before coming onto the views of the proponent of an argument. This was characteristic of most ancient cultures and was not absent in Indian culture. Nor was it imported from the West in colonial times as is often assumed, dissent being linked to European philosophy. Dissent was and is an essential step in the advancement of knowledge. Research and discovery in the pursuit of knowledge are dependent on questioning the explanations that we are given about the world we live in, when we are not convinced about the given explanations, or when we are additionally curious.

From 'Romila Thapar on the History of Dissent and How it Shaped Hinduism and India', interview by Rohan Venkataramakrishnan, *Scroll.in* (31 October 2020) (available online: http://rb.gy/7h750).

The consciousness and role of dissent, it seemed to me, was not sufficiently recognized in studies of the Indian past coming up to the Indian present. I had referred to it in some of my earlier research, but this time around, I wanted to make a statement about the recognition of the concept as significant to various schools of thought and activity in the Indian past, as a prelude to its being significant to the present. It is a subject that historians have tended to marginalize and those that write on culture—with a few exceptions—have virtually ignored. Indian culture is presented as a seamless whole, whereas some of its most illuminating aspects have come from moments of questioning. The *Upanishads*, for example, are an exemplar of the creativity of asking questions.

Why is it important for us to situate dissent in the building of Indian culture? Is that something you think our broader understanding of history—even in academic spaces— lacks?

Dissent is multifaceted. In the examples I have discussed, I have only spoken of its manifestation in a few aspects, limited to very few traditions. Since it is both in dialogue with and parallel to what is maintained by established authority, a full treatment would require many volumes. In any case, my intention in writing this essay was to show, with a few examples, how dissent arises and the creativity that results from its dialogue where it disagrees with existing thought and practice, or else how it carries forward ideas that may seem dormant. It reveals much more in the present.

It is important to the understanding of any culture that its history never was, and can never be, a narrow, restricted movement from the past to the present, and that at no point was it questioned by those who were part of it. When the Shramanas—Buddhists, Jainas, Ajivikas—questioned Vedic Brahmanism, there followed a long period of discussion about the ideas that came out of this questioning. This is reflected not only in the remarkable inscriptions of Ashoka Maurya but also in sections of the *Mahabharata* that were composed at this time. There was also more than a hint of it in the subsequent forms taken by Hinduism, for instance, by some of the Bhakti *sants*. When the Bhakti poet Ravidas describes his vision of a utopia and speaks of a social equality that has no use for caste hierarchies, he is giving form to dissent. This tells us about the priorities of those that control society and those that question it. But these aspects don't often find a place in the teaching of social history, they remain religious texts whose implicit views about society are seldom commented upon analytically.

The book sketches out dissent as it played out in the religious landscape in ancient and medieval India before moving to anti-colonial dissent and then the sort of criticism of the government that is now labelled 'anti-national'.

Why did you draw on this path, rather than looking back primarily at political dissent in Indian history?

The idioms in which a society expresses itself change through history. They are not identical from one period to the next. This is in part why researching and writing the history of thought is intellectually so exciting. It's the unfolding of ideas in relation to society and their mutual impact. I chose the idiom of religious ideas for evident reasons. Firstly, there are more texts from the past focusing on this aspect than on others, so one has access to a fair amount of information to observe the interface of consent and dissent. There are not all that many texts from pre-modern India on theories of explanation relating to society and politics. Commentaries were written on the *dharma-shastras*, or there is the oft-quoted text on political economy, the *Arthashastra*. Some of the ideas in the latter have been linked to notions of causality and logic in stating explanations, but these are incidental to the description of a political economy with which the text is primarily concerned. These subjects tend to be discussed in small, scattered segments. This may be the point at which we historians should move on to researching socio-political dissent by combing through a range of texts. Secondly, because of the close intertwining of religion and caste, exploring the religious idiom incorporates, to some extent, the exploration of the social and political as well. These dimensions are often more apparent in dissenting ideas.

Considering how pervasive the binary Hindu–Muslim conception of the Indian past came to be in the colonial era, do you think it was inevitable that the postcolonial states would continue to grapple with these religious nationalisms for decades after?

No, I don't think it was inevitable. I think we should have anticipated it. Hindu nationalism as a concept comes directly out of one among the tenets of the colonial understanding of India, namely, the two-nation theory. The link should have been shown for what it is. Hindutva, as many people have argued, is not Hinduism. We need dissenting opinions to explain the difference. Nor have the successor nations understood the fundamental historical change that came with Independence. I am referring to the emergence of the nation-state, embodying the rights and obligations of the citizen and the state, as embedded in the Constitution. What we are moving towards, however, and some would say we are already there, is a nation that prioritizes those that are of the religion of the majority and those that assert citizenship rights through their wealth and status. So what has come upon us was predictable.

I remember from my late teens and just after Independence, there was so much animated discussion of the form that Indian society would take as a free nation. It was a vision of social equality and freedom from poverty for all. We are still far away from that.

You mention a few open, unresolved questions about the past, for instance, why there was an upsurge in Krishna bhakti in medieval North India, including among highly placed Muslims. What do you think understanding this better might tell us, particularly about how we use labels and understand the past?

We have to learn not to impose the creations of the present on the past and to recognize how the past looked at itself at various points of time. For example, when we speak about medieval society at large, we make generalizations asserting that 'the Muslims' did this and 'the Hindus' did that, and then draw conclusions from these generalizations about Muslims and Hindus. Our ancestors, however, were far more precise than we are in identifying the communities they were speaking of. They would refer to Yavanas, Shakas, Turushkas and Sufis, keeping in mind their patterns of living, and far less often to 'the Muslims'. Similarly, they referred to Shaivas, Vaishnavas, Shaktas and *nastikas*, and so on, keeping in mind similar indices, rather than calling them 'the Hindus', which was in any case a term that came into use much later.

We have to understand that communities within larger configurations acted in diverse ways. It is these diversities that frequently throw light on how we comprehend people. It is not that all Muslims became Krishna *bhakats*, but only some, and among them a few were highly placed and others were of lower status. Here was a category that was distanced from both the *brahmanas* as well as the *mullahs* and *qazis*, because it was dissenting from the orthodox practice of both. Yet, today, when the poems of such Krishna *bhaktas* are sung as part of the repertoire of Hindustani classical music, few are aware of this dimension and of all its contemporary nuances. That they were part of the upsurge, albeit a small part, implies that there was more than an upsurge in religion, and we have to track how it affected society in a variety of ways.

One thing that occurred to me as I was reading the book was how much the ruling majority in India uses the grammar of this dissenting past albeit, against its own villains, imagined or otherwise—the liberal elite, the deep state, Western powers, Islam, etc.—with Modi as the renouncer. Do you think the Right is tapping into the same tradition that you see existing in the Indian populace?

No, I don't think the Right is aware of the dimensions of this tradition of dissent in the way that I am referring to them, and is therefore not tapping into it. There is little of a secular Right in India today, and the religious Right, largely supporters of Hindutva, have little use for the renunciation that I am speaking of. They tend, in any case, to confuse it with asceticism, whereas I am making a distinction between the two. When they combine, as they occasionally do, the symbols of renunciation with politics, public attention gets directed to the political activity rather than the other, as is demonstrated by the *yogis*, *sadhavis*, etc. who are active members of a political party, and whose political role is most relevant. The political support that is given by the heads of Hindu institutions is a far cry from the tradition of the renouncers.

The renouncer has to locate himself / herself outside society or on its margins, which no one from these organizations does or probably would even consider doing. When the renouncer plays an active social role, his moral authority has to be acknowledged, not his political or administrative office. Gandhi had the moral authority of the renouncer, hence the effectiveness of the techniques of dissent he adopted. This kind of Right would not follow the tradition that I am referring to as it is neither committed to conceding the equality of all Indians—and that implies the utmost tolerance—nor to refraining from violence against those with whom it differs. In the tradition of dissent that I have written about, no one, but no one, would demand that those seen as 'the Other' should be shot dead.

What misconception in our understanding of dissent in India's past do you find yourself most frequently combatting?

As a historian, I would say that what my generation of historians has been trying to combat, and which has been revived in the last few years, is two things: one is the insistence on converting Indian history into, in effect, the history of the majority community; and two, a constant dismissal of incorporating into the study of history new information from various sources and new methods of inquiry and analysis. The intellectual requirements for a serious study of history are dismissed, and history remains an uncertain narrative largely unchanged from that of a century ago. For example, most events of medieval history are explained through the lens of religious hostility between Muslims and Hindus, with the marginalization of any other explanation that might even question this, leave alone disprove this. So we are back once more to repeating the colonial interpretation of Indian history, something that we had begun to question and discard in the last phase of colonial rule. The general anti-intellectualism that is being currently encouraged will inevitably result in discouraging the asking of questions and leave us with a poverty of thought. There is a need to intellectually nourish the rich, diverse, complex and sophisticated explanations that historians have been providing in the last half-century, in a variety of new ways of thinking. Nor will this closure be restricted to historical writing. We are all well aware of what has happened in parallel situations in other countries.

2. *With Charmy Harikrishnan for the* Economic Times

You say Gandhi's nationalism was essentially different from Hindu / Muslim religious nationalism—even when they were fighting colonialism. Is religious nationalism a lesser form of nationalism because it excludes / dominates certain sections?

Gandhi's nationalism was anti-colonial and secular, therefore quite different from Hindu and Muslim nationalism. His support was not drawn from the identity of a single religious community. Nationalism is defined as an identity that is all-inclusive and draws in people of all communities. Therefore, some hesitate to use the term when it is qualified by religion or language or ethnicity, or any single identity. The religious nationalisms—Hindu and Muslim—kept away from anti-colonial nationalism. Their constituency was not and is not the entire citizenry but only a section of it and as defined by a particular religious identity.

You warn against nationalism taking the form of majoritarianism. Do you fear that could happen in India?

From 'There's Now One More Category of Minorities—Indians Who Are Targeted Because They Dissent: Romila Thapar', interview by Charmy Harikrishnan, *Economic Times* (23 October 2020) (available online: http://rb.gy/iu3wd).

An appeal is made to majoritarian religious nationalism in the ideology of the Hindu Rashtra. When physical violence is used in lynching other Indians or calling for them to be shot dead, this cannot be called nationalism. This is anti-nationalism. We now have to add to the religious minorities yet another category—the Indians who are targeted because they dissent. These are generally the better-educated, liberal intellectuals, who are professionals and concerned with defending the rights of Indian citizens. They are not questioning the existence of the nation, they are questioning the methods of governance. Nevertheless, they have been accused of being anti-national and are in jail.

One of the greatest expressions of dissent in recent times was the protest against the Citizenship (Amendment) Act, 2019. Why do you say Shaheen Bagh is in the tradition of Gandhi's Satyagraha?

It was non-violent and committed to avoiding violence of any kind. It was dignified and civilized. It was a protest by that section of society which is treated as subordinate, namely, women, and then too women from the less privileged sections of society. That these women should be protesting is most significant. Their demand was not anti-national, nor was it inciting people to riot, nor was it backed by terrorism, nor was it asking the mob to shoot dead other Indians, nor was it making impossible demands. What they were requesting was a dialogue with the government on the anxieties they felt regarding the legislation relating to the Citizenship (Amendment) Act (CAA), National Register of Citizens (NRC) and National Population Register (NPR). There was and continues to be a widespread debate on this subject among many others.

What does it mean when the state turns dissenters into anti-nationals? What should the state do when citizens express dissent?

I have made a distinction between dissent as an expression of disagreement, and protest that endorses the use of violence to support a demand and which is not therefore identical with dissent. A request that the government discuss the anxieties of citizens over the legislation in question is not an anti-national activity. This is the kind of dialogue that is normal to democratic functioning. Governments often forget that they are elected primarily to represent the people and ensure their rights. Where there is disagreement, there has to be dialogue.

3. With Salim Yusufji for NewsClick

Your choice of theme—tracing patterns of dissent in Indian history—is both heartening and counterintuitive. It would have been more conventional to investigate the roots of our present crisis. How did you decide on this very different course, a hope-instilling take on history? Did you deliberately reject the other option?

I wouldn't describe it as counterintuitive, not at all. On the contrary, I was using examples to show that dissent is not something that we are inventing—or should I say 'constructing'—in our times. This counter-narrative or counter-culture, which I had hinted at some decades ago, clarifies that the notion of an entirely harmonious past does not represent the past. I am not arguing that we should delve deeper into our past to solve our present troubles, but rather that we should ascertain the practice of questioning as it existed in the past. I am not saying that we should do as the past did, but suggesting that understanding how dissent was articulated in the past may perhaps give us some insight into how it can be used in the present. I have tried to explain the success of the *satyagraha* of Gandhi by arguing along these lines. If we get an insight from this, it may help us to better understand the present. Those of us who argued for.

From 'A History of Dissenting Ideas', interview by Salim Yusufji, *NewsClick* (21 November 2020) (available online: http://rb.gy/0wvko).

asking such questions were dismissed as being ideologically prejudiced or imposing modern ideas on the past.

In modern Europe, there was an awareness of the history of dissenting ideas presented in various debates. It was therefore assumed that established ideas can and often do meet with dissent. This is commonly the case in many societies, India included. What we have come to call 'the Indian heritage', in its broadest terms, was being constructed during the last three centuries, as was much that was described as the Indian past. This was first enunciated by colonial perceptions of the past and then by nationalist opinion that tended to accept many—but not all—of the main colonial perceptions. Dissent as a procedure in philosophical thinking was noted, but there was doubt, if not denial, in recognizing its presence in religious and social thinking. Nationalism further discouraged the suggestion that there might have been some conflicting strands in religious and social thought. Early India was projected preferably as a seamless harmonious whole endorsed by the entire society.

I first started writing about dissenting ideas in early India half a century ago. I was mainly interested in dissent as articulated by various groups of Shramanas, such as Buddhists, Jainas and Ajivikas. I argued that renunciation (among other features) was a form of positing an alternate society or at least a society that had different ethical and religious ideals from those characterizing Brahmanism, taken as the prevalent religion. One has to indicate the presence of dissent before one can examine the process of how it gained legitimacy.

You have charted the progress of dissent in multiple strands, and of a mainstream engagement with it that used varying tacks—appropriation, contest, damnation. Yet, in the way you characterize the mainstream in ancient India, the Self is centred upon Sanskrit sources. Why not Prakrit Selves, with Sanskrit as the Other? Right down to the modern period, expressions of conservatism and dissent in your telling are largely religious or framed by religious concepts. Why is it so?

My intention was not to write a history of dissent in India or to discuss the entire range of dissenting views. That would take many volumes and require many authors. My concern was limited to indicating that there has been an expression of dissent in relation to various views taken as established, even in earlier times. It would help if we recognized this and understood it. I therefore chose just a few diverse examples, the more obvious forms of dissent that have not received adequate attention. They lay in the interface between religion and society. They are significant because when a religion is not limited to personal worship alone, but also constructs institutions that seek to control society, then dissent becomes more likely, as happened in India. Such dissent may in part be questioning theology, but more importantly, it also links its questions to social concerns. Shramanism, for example, was at one level a theological disagreement with Vedic Brahmanism, but it also raised questions relating to the social ethic of Brahmanism, thus presenting another perspective on society. As long as it was a theological dispute, the *brahmanas* objected to the Shramanas as *nastikas*, non-believers. When the Shramanas built institutions such as monasteries and intervened more directly in social functioning, the dissent took on other dimensions.

One of the themes that I emphasize in this book is that Indian religion was misunderstood by colonial scholarship. I am not referring to the complaint that Indian religion should have been lauded for its spirituality, tolerance, non-violence, and so on—what may also be found in most other religions and thus need not necessarily be characteristic. I am referring to Indian religion's close interface with social forms that provided it with a forceful social imprint, which appears to have been more effective than in other religions, and which was exercised in varied ways, including the multiplicity of sects and their dialogue as well as their links with caste groups. This was overlooked in colonial formulations of what was described as Hinduism. The religion was presented as yet another unitary, monolithic, belief system. However, it was not another version of the Abrahamic religions. It had diverse intentions and ways of functioning that need investigation.

Among these was the interface of religion and social functioning, where the particular characteristics of each were significant. The obvious example is the weaving together of caste and religious belief and practice. This is present interestingly in almost all the religions practiced in India, even if it is absent in the practice of those established elsewhere in the world such as Islam and

Christianity. In giving attention to dissent in a religious idiom, I was not using religion as an isolated entity in itself, but as an idiom of many aspects of Indian society.

In more recent times, my interest surfaced from observing the form of dissent in the Indian anti-colonial movement—in particular, the Non-Cooperation and Civil Disobedience movement—and how they incorporate the need to protest in a non-violent manner by affecting the functioning of governance and by focusing on the centrality of freedom. I was therefore interested in earlier forms of dissent and whether this anti-colonial form had antecedents. This stemmed from Gandhi using *satyagraha*. Much intellectually evocative and sensitive writing has described the sources that influenced his thought and how he put his ideas together. But that was not my central concern. I was asking another question: why was there such an immense and spontaneous response to the idea of *satyagraha* as encapsulating protest. Dissent does not depend only on the people at the forefront of questioning the world they live in. It also requires a response from those who support the questioning.

On the question of the language of the sources that I have referred to, the first example of the *dasi-putra brahmanas* uses Sanskrit sources. The second example of the Shramanas as dissenting groups is based on the Pali texts from the Buddhist tradition and the Prakrit texts of the Jainas. In my third example, the compositions I refer to are largely in earlier forms of modern Indian languages, such as Braj. In the extensive use of vernacular languages from the fifteenth century onwards, the role of the Persian language and related texts is more complicated.

It would be difficult to locate a period of history when Prakrit was the language of the Self and Sanskrit the language of the Other, for obvious reasons. In the first millennium AD, Buddhists and Jainas also wrote in Sanskrit, in part responding to philosophical debate. The Prakrit or even Pali tradition was not consistently against the Sanskrit Self as it had the Self within its own traditions to contend with. It does not help if we ascribe languages to the status of the Self or the Other, as the status of languages and their use depends on many factors, such as what is being written in the languages, whom do the authors represent, who are the audiences, and what is the social and historical context of the subjects at issue.

You end the book with your visit to Shaheen Bagh and sitting with the women protestors there. You say it revived a sense of the Independence movement. But it was many steps removed from that time. Would you talk about the ways in which Shaheen Bagh expressed to you what has been accomplished since Independence?

Yes, it did bring back memories of the gatherings associated with the anti-colonial national movement of the 1940s. I was not saying that it was a repeat, because there is a great distance in time and context. But there was a certain ambience that had a familiar feel to it and that evoked an earlier age. The anti-colonial mass movement had reached out to women as well, and the 1940s saw their greater participation. They came to the prayer meetings called by Gandhi and to other political gatherings. Women had participated earlier but there was something in the mood of the early forties that was different. Perhaps it was the instinctive feeling that the movement was reaching its pivotal moment—the point of gaining freedom and India becoming an independent nation. The participation of women was impressive, although some have argued that a large number could have been drawn into actively participating in the national movement. It was the recognition that women were required to do more than picketing liquor shops and wearing *khadi*. Participation meant attending meetings and adding their voice to the protest.

It also meant the surfacing of other features that were very much in the air at that time. These features were also reflected in the Shaheen Bagh movement. For a start, it was an entirely non-violent protest, with the women understanding fully well the intention of the movement. They were aware of their constitutional rights as citizens of India, hence the fear of losing this citizenship. Reading repeatedly the Preamble to the Constitution was symbolic of an emphasis on citizenship of a secular kind. It was reminiscent of the kind of citizenship that some of the national leaders of those times were envisioning. The call to women to come out and participate in a political action was a direct confrontation with patriarchy. For patriarchy requires women to be sequestered in the home and not take part in public life.

Equally important, the stand taken by the women was a far cry from communal politics. The immediate concern may have been that the people whose citizenship was being questioned were in the main Muslims. The protestors were asking for a dialogue to discuss the implications of the new laws for their citizenship. On the face of it, the minorities were likely to be the only ones that would be most affected, but, as it turns out, a number of people from the majority community do not have the required documents. It takes on the problematic not just of community identity but Indian identity itself, given the requirement to prove Indian citizenship.

I should perhaps also mention that, for those of us who have a memory of the British Raj and the anti-colonial movement, there is an element of *déjà vu* in some of the events of present times. The debates regarding religious codes controlling freedom of thought and expression that some have been objecting to as an unwanted intervention in the functioning of society, and an undermining of secularism, present a situation that echoes a similar debate that hovered—although more marginally—over the movement for Independence.

Interestingly these attempts to forefront religious controls on society, described as a return to indigenous ways of thinking and acting, are actually rooted in the theories and explanations that were established by colonial governance. For example, the tenacity with which some of the Indian middle class holds onto the British-made two-nation theory. Colonial theories whose inaccuracies my generation tried to expose are returning in forms supported by the patronage of those in authority. These theories are unacceptable to professional historians whose explanations of the past are based on reasoned thinking and logical connections. Reminiscent of colonial actions, dissenting opinion is made punishable using the still-prevalent colonial laws—sedition, for example—in relation to the freedom of expression. When echoes of colonialism surface and people protest, one is inevitably taken back to memories of pre-1947.

The court and the university have not proved a bulwark against attacks on democracy. As deliberative institutions that are much idealized and staffed by some of the most highly trained people in the country, their failure reflects poorly on post-Independence values and priorities. Would you agree?

The court and the university have not been a bulwark against attacks on democracy, but I don't think that this reflects poorly on post-Independence values and priorities. It reflects on those who constitute courts, universities and similar institutions. It reflects on our inability to explain to the public that these institutions are crucial to the functioning of society. We built them without strong foundations. We were perhaps satisfied with merely having these institutions rather than ensuring that they were properly rooted. One could point to a range of factors that stilled the vision of a society moving forward. I shall mention only one aspect from among those that I think were and are crucial.

The change from a colony to an independent nation-state is a fundamental historical change. It involves not just the creation of a nation, and the writing of a constitution to embody that change, both of which we did, but also planning new structures to replace the old ones, at least those that are redundant for the new post-colonial society being envisaged. This last we did not do. We kept adapting colonial institutions to our needs where we should have been working with new ideas and institutions. Some of this was attempted in the first two decades but it faded after that. This has been a critical factor in other post-colonial nations.

The fundamental change entails not just the introduction of the nation-state that represents the nation, but also the creation of the free citizen. Those who were earlier the subjects of authority are now to be independent citizens with rights that ensure their wellbeing. These rights have to be guaranteed by the state to which the citizens in return have some obligations. When I mention rights, I mean the entire gamut, from providing human needs of food, water, health and educational facilities to affirming the equality of all citizens in the functioning of society and therefore social justice. We established the state envisioned as a secular democracy but allowed both qualifiers to gradually weaken. Globalization held out short cuts. The discerning few warned against its economic promises but were not heeded. The potential of the state–citizen relationship establishing a secular democracy is now threatened by religious majoritarianism. This changed situation calls for new thinking.

4. With *Sudipta Datta for the* Hindu

Can there be any advance in knowledge without questioning the world we live in?

No, there cannot be an advance in knowledge if we don't question the world we live in. The intensity and range goading the questioning varies. Questions can be meaningful or not, therefore answers are open to discussion. Disallowing questions is a way of destabilizing society and dismantling institutions.

That dissent was an essential component of civilization is evident from the histories of civilizations. They register a high point in philosophical thinking, new visible forms, new literature. This process draws on questioning what is known—accumulations from the past—and providing creative solutions.

It was earlier thought that civilizations were unique, self-contained and that they advanced in isolation. Now we know to the contrary that cultures tend to be porous. The cutting edge of knowledge requires extensive interaction across civilizations. For example, in the late first millennium AD, there began an impressive exchange of knowledge among astronomers and mathematicians across Eurasia. This encouraged new questions with

From 'The Dissent of Shaheen Bagh Was Visible and Non-violent: Romila Thapar', interview by Sudipta Datta, *The Hindu* (10 October 2020) (available online: http://rb.gy/okiz5).

improved explanations, often leading to new technologies that introduced social change. The astrolabe, for instance, eased maritime navigation and this in turn impacted trade in Eurasia.

Why is it important to make voices on non-violent dissent, for example, the women of Shaheen Bagh, more audible? Why does it remind you of Gandhi and his satyagraha call?

Voices of dissent are more powerful if there is no accompanying violence that can be used to dismiss it. Violence, whatever its source, breeds fear and terror and escalates into uncontrollable disaster. Dissenters generally draw on moral authority rather than violence. When those representing the state lose their moral authority, they may resort to violence in trying to silence dissent. We faced it in the time of the Emergency. Many ask whether it is surfacing again.

I think of the 'activists' accused of inciting riots in association with the 2018 Bhima Koregaon meeting, some of whom were jailed two years ago and now a few more have been added. There has been no trial. There is no habeas corpus. They were not present at the site and gave no public speeches. They worked a long distance away in support of social justice where required. Yet others known to make public speeches urging their audience to shoot dead the citizens of a particular religious identity remain untouched by the same upholders of authority. Discrimination breeds greater fear and terror of authority.

You ask me why today I am reminded of Gandhi and his times and consequently my young days. Fear of authority evokes earlier occasions as when people initially feared the British Raj, a fear that Gandhi and the other leaders had to dispel. They provided an alternative way for people to assert their presence—non-violent dissent—taking form as *satyagraha*. We used to attend the public meetings of anti-colonial nationalists. I still thrill to the slogans that resounded at these meetings of *inquilab zindabad* and *le ke rahenge azadi*. Dissent had to have visibility, but had to be non-violent. And the dissent of Shaheen Bagh was visible and non-violent.

5. With *Sandip Roy for the* Indian Express

I took up the example of dissent as it relates to religious ideas and forms because such dissent stands out quite clearly and yet has not been commented upon sufficiently.

My first example is from the Vedic compositions which refer to the *dasi-putrah brahmanas*, i.e. *brahmanas* who are sons of *dasis*. These were persons inducted from a socially and culturally separate group that appears to be alien, and potentially dissenting. They are at first rejected as being of alien origin, but when they demonstrate their power, they are accepted.

The relevant questions are: Why were they inducted and given the highest status? Was it to appropriate their knowledge? Or to prevent them from dissenting? In the *Mahabharata*, for example, there is also such a person, Vidura, who is almost integrated into the family and is associated with giving sage advice. But he is never given status.

The question often asked is how does Hinduism differ from the Abrahamic religions? To begin with, Abrahamic religions have catechisms and/or creeds of

---

From 'Romila Thapar on Dissent in India from Vedic Brahmanism to Shaheen Bagh', interview by Sandip Roy, *The Sandip Roy Show* (ep. 60) on *The Indian Express* (4 October 2020) (available online: http://rb.gy/066rs).

belief that give a structure to the religion, and dissent lies in questioning them. These are absent in what we call Hinduism or the Shramanic religions. The latter have a mythology and forms of worship that involve multiple deities. The rituals are determined both by worship and by caste. Non-*brahmanas* generally do not perform Brahmanical rituals for those outside of caste.

Hinduism is open to many forms of worship. Bhakti *sants* did not focus on temple worship and congregations were not required. Devotees had their own choice of deity and its icon, or none at all. In some ways, it is the rituals of the caste that one belongs to that are important, or alternatively the denial of caste. The *bhakt* could be of any religion, formal conversion of any kind was not required. Among the more ardent Krishna *bhaktas* were Ras Khan and Rahim Khan-i-Khanan. Some Sufi sects in the Panjab exchanged ideas with Hindu sects such as the Nath yogis. These would all be dissidents in the eyes of orthodox Islam and orthodox Brahmanism.

Dissent in relation to caste was subtler and less obvious. Generally, the facade of *varna* rules was observed, although the activities of a *varna* could change and include those not permitted earlier. For example, *brahmanas* who traded in horses and accumulated enough wealth to make donations to temples were taking up an unexpected occupation. There is more direct dissent from those of the lower castes, such as Kabir, Dadu, and

Raidas. But dissent relating to *varna* is projected in a religious idiom, perhaps because this idiom was the most immediate and could reach all castes.

Whether Hindutva is a form of dissent raises interesting questions. It has forms suggesting dissent, but its intention is not to create an alternate society underlining social ethics, but to return to a presumed utopia for Hindus. This is projected in orthodox terms. But the definitions, although new, do not contradict Hindu belief.

A major innovation is a twist in the territorial factor of the definition. The ancestry of the Hindu has to be from the subcontinent as also the religious belief. Territory also links it to one aspect of nationalism since the latter is given a territorial boundary.

The idea of a Hindu state—Hindu Rashtra—was invented and sustained initially by a group of *brahmanas*. As a political ideology, which is what it essentially is, it drew in part from the Abrahamic religions, especially the imprint of monolithic religion and its advantages. It aims at intensifying the established Hinduism by reformulating it. It is not opposed to Hindu orthodoxy but wants to reformulate it to make it politically effective. It is therefore not a dissenting movement, but one that uses the existing religion as an instrument of political control. This has been effectively demonstrated in the Ramjanmabhoomi movement that destroyed the Babri Masjid.

Is there evidence of dissent in relation to civil society in the early Indian texts?

One cannot go through the whole roster of texts to answer this question, but to do so briefly, let me consider a few.

Where civil society is concerned, the most detailed text is the *Arthashastra*. The assumption of the author is that a properly governed kingdom will not produce dissenters. Nevertheless, they may appear in certain areas for particular reasons. Thus, in newly settled areas, the king should deny entry to renouncers—clearly renouncers associated with the Shramana religions, were recognized as dissenters. This applied more fully to men. Thus, nuns are not given any respect, and it is said that they can be used as spies by the government.

Curiously little is said about the Shramanas. There is no mention of monastic establishments, although there were numerous monasteries built all over as archaeology has revealed and texts have mentioned. Probably dissent in religious thought was a little more acceptable as long as it did not disturb caste rituals and observances.

Another oft-quoted form of civil dissent is peasant revolts. Peasant discontent is mentioned, but more frequently in Shramanic texts. The solution was generally that peasants migrated to the neighbouring kingdom. This is feared by kings as it means a loss of revenue. This assumes there was enough land for new settlements. It was non-violent. Unlike China, peasant revolts are rarely mentioned. The Kaivarta revolt is taken by some historians as a peasant revolt and by others as an uprising of the lesser feudatories in Bengal, in the early second millennium AD.

The assassination of an evil ruler is referred to and preferably done by a person of appropriate caste. An assassination by a *brahmana* would seemingly be regarded as a legitimate form of punishment. In Buddhist texts, the god Indra is said to be involved.

There are references to assassinations of rulers such as the Mauryan king Brihadratha who was assassinated by the *brahmana* Pusyamitra Shunga, the commander of his army, who then usurped the throne.

The question sometimes asked is whether Gandhi changed our idea of revolt, and if so, how did this change catch on. My argument is that Gandhi did not invent an entirely new idea of dissent, but that his *satyagraha* was, at one level, a continuation of the existing ideas of dissent. His use of these ideas came from many sources, Indian and non-Indian. These sources have been discussed at length by many people. My argument is that the acceptance of these forms, as a way of expressing dissent, was familiar to Indians and was readily recognized by them as dissent. That may explain in part why he had such an immense response.

All governments were and are apprehensive about dissent and have to learn to relate to it. It is feared in societies where it takes an active form and becomes violent.

We see so much of it around us in the world these days. But its form and its idiom changes with historical change.

Prior to the emergence of the concept of the rights of citizens, the expression of dissent was guarded. For example, Aryabhatta propounded the theory of the earth going around the sun; it was generally discussed among astronomers, with some agreeing and some disagreeing. In Christian Europe, the theory had to be suppressed until it was safe to discuss it publicly. So there are historical moments for the acceptance or the rejection of ideas.

Now with the endorsement of the rights of citizens to disagree with institutions of government—even if only in theory in some societies—those in authority should be more careful about suppressing dissent. However, rights are never God-given—they have to be struggled for and have to be guarded so that they don't get swept away. This is where agencies involved in the governance of a society have a central role, for instance, the judiciary that is the ultimate protector of these rights. In order to be the protector, it must have the stature of an independent institution, it must be autonomous and especially so as the guardian of rights. It loses its reason to exist if it becomes an arm of government.

Similarly with institutions that support social functioning. They have to take care to maintain their autonomy. The police and the bureaucracy, for instance, that are part of the executive working of governance have to constantly keep in mind that their work is to protect citizens, not to terrorize them. They have constantly to be reminded that the work they are doing is essentially to ensure the welfare of the citizen, and not merely to carry out the wishes of whichever government is ruling. They are not dealing with the inferior subjects of the British Raj, but with fellow Indians with full rights. Nor are they agencies to propagate the ideology of whoever constitutes government.

We may well ask whether this is something we have forgotten in our seventy-six years of Independence, or have we failed to retrain these institutions to remove the colonial imprint in their functioning and direct themselves to the welfare of citizens?

The rights of citizens did not exist in pre-modern times. They come with the nation-state and accompany the change from a person being a subject of the state— the *praja*, the child—to being a free citizen. This is a fundamental change that we seem not to have even recognized leave alone made. The rights need to be asserted so that they are easily recognized and can be exercised. The function of governance is to propagate and defend the rights of citizens, not to decimate them. That's what democracy is all about.

Closing the channels of dialogue indicates either a lack of confidence among those governing, or else a fear of dissenting groups. Channels of dialogue get closed when the essential institutions of democracy are subverted and made ineffectual, in particular universities and media outlets. Then a point comes when the controls can and do backfire—anti-colonial movements are recent examples.

It has been asked whether the present discomfort with dissent reflects a disregard for learning and intellectual inquiry. My answer is yes. We now have a middle class, a large part of which has stopped inquiring and thinking. It is content to pick up what media of various kinds say as well as the crude opinion of an army of trolls planted everywhere. Intelligent media just about exists but is waning. Anti-intellectualism is evident from the official projects, programmes and policies that more often than not reflect out-of-date knowledge, by the systematic suffocation of universities and institutions doing new kinds of research and by imprisoning lawyers, academics and writers for a long period without trial.

Take for example my discipline, history. The official history that is now being introduced is history according to the requirements of Hindutva, rooted in colonial readings that were abandoned by historians a century ago. They may well succeed in marginalizing the history of historians or even burying it, but they cannot understand that this is a pointless exercise as there will be enough intellectuals in India and elsewhere seeking answers to complex questions who will read the historians' histories—even if they are being written surreptitiously! So textbooks will change in the immediate present and they will popularize their legitimacy from the past that Hindutva is desperately seeking. But there will always be the alternate history waiting to be read with greater eagerness than before.

Politicians should be reminded that it is not they who make history—as they assume. The historians make history. It is the historians who select what is to be remembered and how it is to be interpreted. So despite the wish to replace history by fantasy, history will actually remain secure. A case in point is the Nazi attempt in Germany to write German history as that of a pure Aryan race. Today, this history has been trashed. The other obvious parallel is that of the Cultural Revolution in China. A new history became the source of knowledge. Within a decade and under the severest thought control, it was slowly edged out and the more substantial history returned.

How effective is dissent in present times?

Dissent is not expressed in a hurry. It requires to be thought about carefully and the most effective way of expressing it has to be worked out. Dissent also requires to be pronounced by persons with moral authority in order to attract support for the right reasons. This we have learnt from past teachers who dissented—the Shramanas and some of the Bhakti *sants* and Sufis. In a sense, that is why dissent has to be non-violent and civilized. Dissent is after all pitching moral authority against the physical authority and the institutional authority of those whose views are the cause of the dissent.

Where today will we find the moral authority? Will the Indian middle class still respond to those who are imbued with a sense of ethics with a concern to improve the human condition of all Indians irrespective of their identities? Or has the majoritarian ideology taken over to ensure that ethics and humanism are no longer the crucial concern. Is it now every Indian for himself—by hook or by crook. All that matters are money and power and this is to be obtained by any means.

As a historian, I often turn to the past these days. I console myself for present conditions by thinking of past happenings, such as the anti-colonial movement that gave us such immense strength. We did not use this strength to advocate the shooting of other Indians. We used it to think analytically about the society that we wished to create as a free nation. Some had even begun to work towards such an improved society. Or else, I try and convince myself that nightmares are transient, however unending they may seem when one is asleep. Occasionally there is a small flash from the future and I begin to hope . . .

6. With Suchitra Vijayan for the Polis Project

How did the labels of 'Hindu' and 'Muslim' emerge?

The labels of 'Hindu' and 'Muslim' to identify uniform monolithic religions and identities were adopted only later in about the fifteenth century. Their usage increased during colonial times when they were made the main signifiers of identity.

'Hindu' is initially a geographical label used by those in West Asia to refer to the land and people of al-Hind, that is, the territory across the Indus or Sindhu. Around the mid-second millennium AD, it began to be applied for the first time to those who were not Muslims or Christians. In Sanskrit texts largely authored by *brahmanas*, the term *nastika* was used to differentiate those who were not following the *brahmana* beliefs and codes. The *nastikas* now included not only the Buddhists and Jainas as in earlier times, but also the Turushkas or Turks from Central Asia who had by now converted to Islam. As non-believers, they had the low social status of *mleccha* even though, as Sultans, they were otherwise treated with deference.

From 'A History of Dissent: A Conversation with Romila Thapar', interview by Suchitra Vijayan, *The Polis Project* (30 September 2020) (available online: http://rb.gy/emgyb).

The colonial perspective projected Indian society as consisting of two nations—the Hindu and the Muslim. The Hindus were everyone except the Muslims and Christians. This was irrespective of the differing belief systems in the sects that were described by the term 'Hindu'. The flexibility of perceiving a religion with its complexities arising from the constituent multiple sects, some linked and some not, was drastically altered in these new definitions.

Nationalism is a historical phase. How would you characterize Indian nationalism today?

Nationalism as a historical phase does not go back to pre-modern times. As a historian, I argue that it is a part of a foundational change in societies, coinciding with capitalism and the emergence of a middle class. It reflects the middle class wishing to control the economy as well as political power and asserting a high status. The nation-state replaces the state system of old, that is, a kingdom with a ruler governing the people regarded as subjects.

Most importantly, what is still not understood in India are the implicit changes. The basic unit is the citizen, and citizens now replace the subjects of old. I use the word replace because there are major differences between subject and citizen. The citizen has important rights guaranteed by the state. There has to be an elected government, representing the citizens and protecting their rights. The rights of the citizens in relation to the state are contracted and recorded in the Constitution, which the government has to obey. The rights apply equally to all citizens with no exceptions.

Nationalism is the ideology that links territory, state and citizens. It is therefore an identity inclusive of all. Nationalism includes every citizen with no qualifications of one identity having priority over the others. This was an issue in the 1930s. Anti-colonial nationalism included every citizen—and a few others as well if they wished it. But religious nationalisms such as the two—the Muslim and the Hindu nationalisms—were exclusive. Nationalism was qualified by religion, and priority was given to members of a particular religious community. This raised the issue of secularism as well. Only the inclusive nationalism could be secular, and was. Religious nationalisms cannot be secular.

When nationalism gives priority to any single identity because it has a majority, then nationalism is replaced by majoritarianism, and this is a negation of democracy. What is called religious nationalism in India, with a priority in citizenship for the Hindu majority, is therefore criticized as not being nationalism.

Can we radically reimagine the nation and the citizen?

This will be necessary if we are to survive as a democratic, secular nation. We shall have to take the historical context seriously and understand what the change to being a nation-state actually means. This is an exercise that we never carried out. We assumed that it would naturally fall into place—almost by default. It might help even if we start now.

We have to take the rights of citizenship far more literally and seriously. To start with, we could suggest that every nation-state must have a foundational layer to which every government, irrespective of the politics of the party in power or its economic policy, must be committed. This would be the guarantee of the rights of the citizens that every state has to provide. It would move from food, water, shelter to employment, healthcare and education, together with equality in citizenship and social justice.

Only when this is ensured and guaranteed, possibly overseen by authority beyond the nation-state, can governments decide where to go next. We have to take the rights of citizenship far more literally and seriously than we have done so far. This will require radical restructuring of the economies in many states but the attraction for those who govern will be the decreased potential of violent protest. We could perhaps start by reminding the departments of government of what they are actually meant to do and not what they happen to be doing. Of course, this change looks undoable in the current situation, but our survival depends on visualizing and activating a better world.

Readings

Prologue

SAID, Edward. *Orientalism: Western Conceptions of the Orient.* New York: Pantheon Books, 1978.

SMART, Ninian. *Doctrine and Argument in Indian Philosophy.* London: Allen and Unwin, 1964.

1

Aitareya Brahmana (A. B. Keith trans.) in *Rigveda Brahmanas: The Aitareya and Kausitaki Brahmanas of the Rigveda.* New Delhi: Motilal Banarsidass, 1996 [London, 1920].

Brihad-devata (M. Tokunaga ed.). Kyoto: Rinsen Book Company, 1997.

CHAKRAVARTI, Uma. 'Whatever Happened to the Vedic *Dasi*: Orientalism, Nationalism and a Script for the Past' in Kumkum Sangari and Sudesh Vaid (eds.), *Recasting Women: Essays in Colonial History.* New Delhi: Kali for Women, 1989, pp. 27–87.

DESHPANDE, Madhav M., and Peter Edwin Hook (eds). *Aryan and Non-Aryan in India.* Ann Arbor, MI: Center for South and Southeast Asian Studies, 1979.

The Principal Upanisads (Sarvepalli Radhakrishnan ed., trans., introd. and annot.). London: Allen and Unwin, 1953.

The Rigveda: The Earliest Religious Poetry of India (Jamison, Stephanie W. and Joel P. Brereton trans). New York: Oxford University Press (South Asia Research Series), 2014. Available online at: https://bit.ly/3mktxnu (last accessed on 3 September 2020).

SINGH, Hira. *Recasting Caste: From the Sacred to the Profane.* New Delhi: Sage, 2004.

STAAL, Frits. *Discovering the Vedas: Origins, Mantras, Rituals, Insights.* New Delhi: Penguin, 2008.

THAPAR, Romila. 'The Archaeological Background to the Agnicayana Ritual' in Romila Thapar, *The Historian and Her Craft, Volume 2.* New Delhi: Oxford University Press, 2017, pp. 92–121.

———. 'Fragmentary Narratives from the *Vedas*' in Romila Thapar, *The Past before Us: Historical Traditions of Early North India.* Ranikhet: Permanent Black, 2013, pp. 87–143.

———, Michael Witzel, Jaya Menon, Kai Friese and Razib Khan (eds), *Which of Us Are Aryans? Rethinking the Concept of Our Origins.* New Delhi: Aleph, 2019.

2

Ancient India as Described by Megasthenés and Arrian; Being a Translation of the Fragments of the Indika of Megasthenés Collected by Dr. Schwanbeck, and of the First Part of the Indika of Arrian (J. W. McCrindle trans., introd. and annot.). Calcutta: Chuckervertty, Chatterje and Co., 1926. Available online at: https://bit.ly/2GOF0eD (last accessed on 3 September 2020).

BANA BHATTA. *The Harsa-Carita of Bana* (E. B. Cowell and F. W. Thomas trans). London, 1929[1897]. Available online at: https://bit.ly/32tKV1b (last accessed on 14 September 2020).

CHATTOPADHYAYA, Debiprasad, *Lokayata: A Study in Ancient Indian Materialism.* New Delhi: People's Publishing House, 1959.

———, and Mrinal Kanti Gangopadhyaya (eds.), *Carvaka/ Lokayata: An Anthology of Source Materials and Some*

Recent Studies. New Delhi: Indian Council of Philosophical Research, 1990.

CHAKRAVARTI, Uma. *Social Dimensions of Early Buddhism*. New Delhi: Oxford University Press, 1987.

DHERE, Ramchandra Chintaman. *The Rise of a Folk God: Vitthal of Pandharpur* (Anne Feldhaus trans.). Delhi: Oxford University Press, 2011.

JAINI, Padmanabh S. *The Jaina Path of Purification*. Berkeley, CA: University of California Press, 1979. Also New Delhi: Motilal Banarsidass, 2014. The latter is available online at: https://bit.ly/2ZRlEwn (last accessed on 3 September 2020).

Kalhana's Rajatarangini: A Chronicle of the Kings of Kashmir, 3 VOLS (M. A Stein trans., introd. and comment.). New Delhi: Motilal Banarsidass, 1979[1900].

The Kautilya Arthasastra, 3 VOLS (R. P. Kangle ed., trans. and comm.). Bombay: University of Bombay (University of Bombay Studies: Sanskrit, Prakrit and Pali, Nos. 1–3), 1960, 1963, 1965, respectively.

Manu's Code of Law: A Critical Edition and Translation of the Manava-dharmasastra (Patrick Olivelle ed. and trans.). New York: Oxford University Press, 2005. [See also *The Law Code of Manu: A New Translation Based on the Critical Edition by Patrick Olivelle* (New York: Oxford University Press, 2004).]

NAGASENA, *Milinda-panho* as: *The Questions of King Milinda*, 2 VOLS (T. W. Rhys Davids trans.). New York: Dover Publications (Sacred Books of the East Series), 1963.

Patanjali's Vyakarana-Mahabhasya (S. D. Joshi ed., trans. and annot.). Poona: University of Poona (Publications of the Centre of Advanced Study in Sanskrit Class C, No. 3), 1968. Available online at: https://bit.ly/2GY1J8i (last accessed on 3 September 2020).

The Puranas (Ludo Rocher trans.). Wiesbaden: Verlag Otto Harrassowitz (History of Indian Literature Series), 1986.

The Sarva-darshana-sangraha or Review of the Different Systems of Hindu Philosophy by Madhava Acharya (E. B. Cowell and A. E. Gough trans). London: Trübner and Co., 1882. Available online at: https://bit.ly/35z94p9 (last accessed on 3 September 2020).

ROY, Kumkum. 'Representing Heresies: The "Others" in the Ekanipata Jataka'. Paper presented at the symposium 'Heresies in History'—Indian History Congress 72nd Session, Patiala, 12 December 2011.

SARAO, K. T. S., *Decline of Buddhism in India: A Fresh Perspective*. New Delhi: Munshiram Manoharlal, 2012.

SHRIMALI, Krishna Mohan. 'Reason and Rationality: Some Leaves from India's Intellectual History'. *Social Scientist* 46 (3–4) (538–539) (March–April 2018): 3–44.

SKILLING, Peter. *Questioning the Buddha*. Somerville, MA: Wisdom Publications, 2021.

SONTHEIMER, Gunther-Dietz. *Pastoral Deities in Western India* (Anne Feldhaus ed. and trans.). New Delhi: Oxford University Press, 1993.

THAPAR, Romila. *Asoka and the Decline of the Mauryas*. New Delhi: Oxford University Press, 1996.

——. 'The *Puranas*: Heresy and the *Vamsanucarita*' in Romila Thapar, *The Historian and Her Craft*, VOL. 4. New Delhi: Oxford University Press, 2017, pp. 184–204.

——. 'Renunciation: The Making of a Counter-Culture?' in Romila Thapar, *The Historian and Her Craft*, VOL. 4. New Delhi: Oxford University Press, 2017, pp. 102–37.

VERARDI, Giovanni. *Hardships and Downfall of Buddhism in India*. Singapore: Institute of Southeast Asian Studies / New Delhi: Manohar, 2011.

WATTERS, Thomas. *On Yuang Chwang's Travels in India, 629–645 AD* (T. W. Rhys Davids, S. W. Bushell and Vincent A. Smith eds.). London: Royal Asiatic Society (Oriental Translation Fund New Series, VOL. XIV), 1904. Available online at: https://bit.ly/33og0mh (last accessed on 3 September).

3

AMBEDKAR B. R. *Annihilation of Caste: An Undelivered Speech* (Mulk Raj Anand ed.). New Delhi: Arnold Publishers, 1990.

DONIGER, Wendy. *Dissent in the Ancient Indian Series of Sex and Politics.* New Haven, CT: Yale University Press, 2018.

ILAIAH, Kancha. *Why I Am Not a Hindu.* Calcutta: Samya Publishers, 1996.

JHA, Vivekanand. *Candala: Untouchability and Caste in Early India.* New Delhi: Primus Books, 2018.

The Mahabharata, Volume 7: Book 11, The Book of the Women, and Book 12, The Book of Peace, Part 1 (J. L. Fitzgerald trans. and introd.). Chicago: The University of Chicago Press, 2004, pp. 79–164.

SHARMA, Ram Sharan. *Sudras in Ancient India: A Social History of the Lower Order Down to Circa A.D. 600,* 2nd REVD EDN. New Delhi: Motilal Banarsidass, 1980 .

ZELLIOT, Eleanor and Rohini Mokashi-Punekar. *Untouchable Saints: An Indian Phenomenon.* New Delhi: Manohar, 2005.

4

BHAGAVAN, Manu and Anne Feldhaus (eds). *Speaking Truth to Power: Religion, Caste and the Subaltern Question in India.* New Delhi: Oxford University Press, 2009.

EATON, Richard M. *India in the Persianate Age: 1000–1765.* New York: Allen Lane, 2019.

ERNST, Carl W. *Refractions of Islam in India: Situating Sufism and Yoga*. New Delhi: Sage, 2016.

ESCHMANN, A. 'Religion, Reaction and Change: The Role of Sects in Hinduism' in Gunther-Dietz Sontheimer and Hermann Kulke (eds), *Hinduism Reconsidered*. New Delhi: Manohar, 1989, pp. 108–20.

FLOOD, Finbar Barry. *Objects of Translation: Material Culture and Medieval 'Hindu–Muslim' Encounter*. Princeton, NJ: Princeton University Press, 2009.

GANGARAM, *The Maharashtra Purana: An Eighteenth Century Bengali Historical Text* (Edward C. Dimock and Pratul Chandra Gupta trans., annot. and introd.). Calcutta: Orient Longman, 1985.

HAWLEY, John Stratton. *A Storm of Songs: India and the Idea of the Bhakti Movement*. Cambridge, MA: Harvard University Press, 2015

———, and Mark Juergensmeyer. *Songs of the Saints of India*. New Delhi: Oxford University Press, 2007.

JAINI, Padmanabh S. 'Jaina Puranas: A Puranic Counter Tradition' in Wendy Doniger (ed), *Purana Perennis: Reciprocity and Transformation in Hindu and Jaina Texts*. New York: SUNY Press, 1993, pp. 207–49.

MADHUSUDANA SARSVATI. *Prasthanabheda*. Srirangam: Sri Vani Vilas Press, 1919 [Sanskrit]. Available online at: https://bit.ly/35y2wXG (last accessed on 3 September 2020).

MUKTA, Parita. *Upholding Common Life: The Community of Mirabai*. New Delhi: Oxford University Press, 1998.

PRASHAD, Pushpa. *Sanskrit Inscriptions of the Delhi Sultanate, 1191–1526*. New Delhi: Oxford University Press, 1990.

TALBOT, Cynthia. 'Inscribing the Other, Inscribing the Self: Hindu–Muslim Identities in Pre-colonial India'. *Comparative Studies in Society and History* 37(4) (1995): 692–722.

The Yuga Purana (John E. Mitchiner ed., trans. and introd.)
Calcutta: The Asiatic Society, 1986. Available online at:
https://bit.ly/3kbV3Sj (last accessed on 3 September 2020).

5

ANDERSON, Benedict. *Imagined Communities: Reflections on the
Origin and Spread of Nationalism*, REVD EDN. London: Verso
2006[1983].

GOLWALKAR, M. S. *We, or Our Nationhood Defined*. Nagpur:
Bharat Publications, 1939.

HOBSBAWM, Eric. *Nations and Nationalism since 1780: Pro-
gramme, Myth, Reality*. Cambridge: Cambridge University
Press, 1990.

JONES, Kenneth W. *Arya Dharm: Hindu Consciousness in 19th-
Century Punjab*. New Delhi: Manohar, 1989.

SAVARKAR, Vinayak Damodar. *Essentials of Hindutva*. Bombay:
Veer Savarkar Prakashan, 1923.

———. *Hindutva: Who Is a Hindu?* Bombay: Veer Savarkar
Prakashan, 1928. Available online at: https://bit.ly/35wDJmU
(last accessed on 3 September 2020).

SCHWAB, Raymond. *La Renaissance Orientale*. Paris: Payot,
1950. Available in English as: *The Oriental Renaissance:
Europe's Rediscovery of India and the East 1680–1880* (Gene
Patterson-Black and Victor Reinking trans; Edward W. Said
foreword). New York: Columbia University Press, 1984.

THAPAR, Romila. 'Imagined Religious Communities: Ancient
History and the Modern Search for a Hindu Identity' in
Romila Thapar, *The Historian and Her Craft*, VOL. 1. New
Delhi: Oxford University Press, 2017, pp. 131–54.

TILAK, Bal Gangadhar. *The Arctic Home of the Vedas: Being Also
a New Key to the Interpretation of Many Vedic Texts and
Legends*. Poona: Tilak Bros., 1909.

6

CHAKRBARTI, Kunal. *Religious Process: the Puranas and the Making of a Regional Tradition.* New Delhi: Oxford University Press, 2001.

DALMIA, Vasudha, and Heinrich von Steitencron (eds). *The Oxford India Hinduism Reader.* New Delhi: Oxford University press, 2007.

KING, Richard. *Orientalism and Religion: Postcolonial Theory, India and 'The Mystic East'.* New Delhi: Routledge, 1999.

LORENZEN, David. *Who Invented Hinduism? Essays on Religion in History.* New Delhi: Yoda Press, 2006.

PENNINGTON, Brian K. *Was Hinduism Invented? Britons, Indians, and the Colonial Construction of Religion.* New York: Oxford University Press, 2005.

SONTHEIMER, Gunther-Dietz, and Hermann Kulke (eds). *Hinduism Reconsidered.* New Delhi: Manohar, 2001.

7

ERIKSON, Erik H. *Gandhi's Truth: On the Origins of Militant Nonviolence.* New York. W. W. Norton, 1969.

GANDHI, Rajmohan. *Why Gandhi Still Matters: An Appraisal of the Mahatma's Legacy.* New Delhi: Aleph, 2017.

HOWARD, Veena R. *Gandhi's Ascetic Activism: Renunication and Social Action.* New York: SUNY Press, 2013.

SKARIA, Ajay. *Unconditional Equality: Gandhi's Religion of Resistance.* New Delhi: Orient Blackswan, 2016.

8

THAPAR, Romila. *The Past before Us: Historical Traditions of Early North India.* Ranikhet: Permanent Black, 2013.

ZEIGLER, Norman P. 'Marvari Historical Chronicles: Sources for the Social and Cultural History of Rajasthan'. *Indian Economic and Social History Review* 13(2) (1976): 219–50.

9

AMIN, Shahid. 'Gandhi as Mahatma: Gorakhpur District, Eastern UP, 1921–22' in Ranajit Guha (ed.), *Subaltern Studies 3: Writings on South Asian History and Society*. New Delhi: Oxford University Press, 1984, pp. 1–61.

BASHAM, A. L. *The Origins and Development of Classical Hinduism* (Kenneth G. Zysk ed.). New Delhi: Oxford University Press, 1991.

FITZGERALD, J. L. 'Introduction' to *The Mahabharata, Volume 7: Book 11, The Book of the Women, and Book 12, The Book of Peace, Part 1* (J. L. Fitzgerald trans. and introd.). Chicago: University of Chicago Press, 2004, pp. 98ff.

HAUSER, Walter. *The Bihar Provincial Kisan Sabha 1929–1942: A Study of an Indian Peasant Movement* (William R. Pinch foreword; curated with an afterword by Kailash Chandra Jha). New Delhi: Manohar, 2019.

PALSHIKAR, Sanjay. *Evil and the Philosophy of Retribution: Modern Commentaries on the Bhagavad-Gita*. New Delhi: Routledge, 2016.

PINCH, William R. *Peasants and Monks in British India*. Berkeley, CA: University of California Press, 1996.

SIDDIQUI, M. H. *Agrarian Unrest in North India: United Provinces, 1918–22*. New Delhi: Vikas Publishing House (Vikas History Series), 1978.

SUKTHANKAR, Vishnu Sitaram. *On the Meaning of the Mahabharata*. Bombay: Asiatic Society of Bombay, 1998[1957].

SUTTON, Nick. 'Asoka and Yudhisthira: A Historical Setting for the Ideological Tensions of the Mahabharata?' *Religion* 27(4) (1997): 333–41.